NATIONAL ACADEMIES *Sciences Engineering Medicine*

NATIONAL ACADEMIES PRESS
Washington, DC

Gilbert W. Beebe Symposium

AI and ML Applications in Radiation Therapy, Medical Diagnostics, and Radiation Occupational Health and Safety

Convened March 13–14, 2025

Daniel Mulrow and Robert Pool, *Rapporteurs*

Nuclear and Radiation Studies Board

Division on Earth and Life Studies

Proceedings of a Symposium

NATIONAL ACADEMIES PRESS 500 Fifth Street, NW Washington, DC 20001

This activity was supported by a contracts from the American College of Radiology, U.S. Department of Energy (Award #DE-EM0005239 and Award #DE-HS0000031), the Gordon and Betty Moore Foundation (Grant ID# 12565), the National Academy of Sciences Thomas Lincoln Casey Fund, the Richard Lounsbery Foundation, and the U.S. Nuclear Regulatory Commission (Award #31310024M0056). Any opinions, findings, conclusions, or recommendations expressed in this publication do not necessarily reflect the views of any organization or agency that provided support for the project.

International Standard Book Number-13: 978-0-309-99459-0
Digital Object Identifier: https://doi.org/10.17226/29200

This publication is available from the National Academies Press, 500 Fifth Street, NW, Keck 360, Washington, DC 20001; (800) 624-6242; https://nap.nationalacademies.org.

The manufacturer's authorized representative in the European Union for product safety is Authorised Rep Compliance Ltd., Ground Floor, 71 Lower Baggot Street, Dublin D02 P593 Ireland; www.arccompliance.com.

Printed in the United States of America.

Suggested citation: National Academies of Sciences, Engineering, and Medicine. 2025. *Gilbert W. Beebe Symposium: AI and ML Applications in Radiation Therapy, Medical Diagnostics, and Radiation Occupational Health and Safety: Proceedings of a Symposium*. Washington, DC: National Academies Press. https://doi.org/10.17226/29200.

The **National Academy of Sciences** was established in 1863 by an Act of Congress, signed by President Lincoln, as a private, nongovernmental institution to advise the nation on issues related to science and technology. Members are elected by their peers for outstanding contributions to research. Dr. Marcia McNutt is president.

The **National Academy of Engineering** was established in 1964 under the charter of the National Academy of Sciences to bring the practices of engineering to advising the nation. Members are elected by their peers for extraordinary contributions to engineering. Dr. Tsu-Jae Liu is president.

The **National Academy of Medicine** (formerly the Institute of Medicine) was established in 1970 under the charter of the National Academy of Sciences to advise the nation on medical and health issues. Members are elected by their peers for distinguished contributions to medicine and health. Dr. Victor J. Dzau is president.

The three Academies work together as the **National Academies of Sciences, Engineering, and Medicine** to provide independent, objective analysis and advice to the nation and conduct other activities to solve complex problems and inform public policy decisions. The National Academies also encourage education and research, recognize outstanding contributions to knowledge, and increase public understanding in matters of science, engineering, and medicine.

Learn more about the National Academies of Sciences, Engineering, and Medicine at **www.nationalacademies.org**.

Consensus Study Reports published by the National Academies of Sciences, Engineering, and Medicine document the evidence-based consensus on the study's statement of task by an authoring committee of experts. Reports typically include findings, conclusions, and recommendations based on information gathered by the committee and the committee's deliberations. Each report has been subjected to a rigorous and independent peer-review process and it represents the position of the National Academies on the statement of task.

Proceedings published by the National Academies of Sciences, Engineering, and Medicine chronicle the presentations and discussions at a workshop, symposium, or other event convened by the National Academies. The statements and opinions contained in proceedings are those of the participants and are not endorsed by other participants, the planning committee, or the National Academies.

Rapid Expert Consultations published by the National Academies of Sciences, Engineering, and Medicine are authored by subject-matter experts on narrowly focused topics that can be supported by a body of evidence. The discussions contained in rapid expert consultations are considered those of the authors and do not contain policy recommendations. Rapid expert consultations are reviewed by the institution before release.

For information about other products and activities of the National Academies, please visit www.nationalacademies.org/about/whatwedo.

SYMPOSIUM PLANNING COMMITTEE[1]

LEO CHIANG (*Co-Chair*), The Dow Chemical Company
SHAHEEN A. DEWJI (*Co-Chair*), Georgia Institute of Technology
CAROLINE CHUNG, The University of Texas MD Anderson Cancer Center
SYLVAIN V. COSTES, National Aeronautics and Space Administration
ANYI LI, Memorial Sloan Kettering Cancer Center
CEFERINO OBCEMEA, National Cancer Institute

National Academies of Sciences, Engineering, and Medicine Staff

DANIEL J. MULROW, Project Director and Program Officer
FRANCIS AMANKWAH, Senior Program Officer
CHARLES D. FERGUSON, Senior Board Director
DARLENE GROS, Senior Program Assistant
LAURA LLANOS, Financial Business Partner

[1] The National Academies of Sciences, Engineering, and Medicine's symposium planning committees are solely responsible for organizing the symposium, identifying topics, and choosing speakers. The responsibility for the published Proceedings of a Symposium rests with the rapporteurs and the institution.

Reviewers

This Proceedings of a Symposium was reviewed in draft form by individuals chosen for their diverse perspectives and technical expertise. The purpose of this independent review is to provide candid and critical comments that will assist the National Academies of Sciences, Engineering, and Medicine in making each published proceedings as sound as possible and to ensure that it meets the institutional standards for quality, objectivity, evidence, and responsiveness to the charge. The review comments and draft manuscript remain confidential to protect the integrity of the process.

We thank the following individuals for their review of this proceedings:

DANIELLE BITTERMAN, Dana-Farber Cancer Institute
SYLVAIN COSTES, National Aeronautics and Space Administration (*former*)
AMANDA SHEHU, George Mason University

Although the reviewers listed above provided many constructive comments and suggestions, they were not asked to endorse content of the proceedings nor did they see the final draft before its release. The review of this report was overseen by **JOE W. GRAY (NAM),** Oregon Health and Science University. He was responsible for making certain that an independent examination of this report was carried out in accordance with the standards of the National Academies and that all review comments were carefully considered. Responsibility for the final content rests entirely with the rapporteurs and the National Academies.

Contents

APPENDIXES

Acronyms and Abbreviations

AAPM	American Association of Physicists in Medicine
ACR	American College of Radiology
AI	artificial intelligence
ARCH-AI	American College of Radiology Recognized Center for Healthcare-AI
ARPA-H	Advanced Research Projects Agency for Health
ART	adaptive radiotherapy
AUTOMAP	Automated Transform by Manifold Approximation
C-HER	Centralized Health and Exposomic Resource
CFR	Council on Foreign Relations
CNN	convolutional neural network
CNSC	Canadian Nuclear Safety Commission
CT	computed tomography
DICOM	Digital Imaging and Communications in Medicine
DNN	deep neural network
eGFR	estimated glomerular filtration rate
EHR	electronic health record
EHRLICH	Electronic Health Record–Informed Lagrangian Method for Precision Public Health
EKG	electrocardiogram
ERR	excess relative risk
FAS	Federation of American Scientists
FDA	Food and Drug Administration
FFR	fractional flow reserve
GDPR	General Data Protection Regulation
GPT	Generative Pretrained Transformer
Gy	gray, unit of absorbed radiation dose

HCI	human–computer interaction
HEDIS	Healthcare Effectiveness Data and Information Set
HITI	Healthcare Artificial Intelligence Innovation and Translational Informatics
J&J	Johnson & Johnson
LLM	large language model
mGy	milligray
MIDRC	Medical Imaging and Data Resource Center
MIT	Massachusetts Institute of Technology
ML	machine learning
MOSSAIC	Making Outcomes Using Surveillance Data and Scalable Artificial Intelligence for Cancer
MR	magnetic resonance
MRI	magnetic resonance imaging
NASA	National Aeronautics and Space Administration
NCI	National Cancer Institute
NICE	National Institute for Health and Care Excellence
NIH	National Institutes of Health
NLP	nonlinear parametric
NRC	Nuclear Regulatory Commission
NRSB	Nuclear and Radiation Studies Board
OCT	optical coherence tomography
PET	positron emission tomography
PINN	physics-informed neural network
PSMA	Prostate-Specific Membrane Antigen
QIB	quantitative imaging biomarker
QIBA	Quantitative Imaging Biomarkers Alliance
QMIC	Quantitative Medical Imaging Coalition
R&D	research and development
RCT	randomized controlled trial
RERF	Radiation Effects Research Foundation
RPT	radiopharmaceutical therapy
SciML	scientific machine learning
SEER	Surveillance, Epidemiology, and End Results
SHAP values	Shapley Additive Explanations
SNR	signal-to-noise ratio
T	tesla, unit of magnetic flux density
UCSD	University of California, San Diego
UNC	University of North Carolina
UT	University of Texas

VA	Veterans Affairs
VVUQ	verification, validation, and uncertainty quantification
XAI	explainable artificial intelligence
ZCTA	zip code tabulation area

1
Introduction

The Gilbert W. Beebe Symposium was established by the Board on Radiation Effects Research (a predecessor of the Nuclear and Radiation Studies Board) in 2002 to honor the scientific achievements of the late Dr. Gilbert W. Beebe, a distinguished National Cancer Institute radiation epidemiologist who was one of the designers and key implementers of the epidemiology studies of Japanese atomic bomb survivors and a co-founder of the Medical Follow-up Agency. Beebe passed away in 2003. The symposium is used to promote discussions among scientists, federal staff, and other interested parties concerned with radiation health effects.

On March 13–14, 2025, the Nuclear and Radiation Studies Board of the National Academies of Sciences, Engineering, and Medicine (National Academies) hosted the most recent Gilbert W. Beebe symposium, with the goal of discussing the applications of artificial intelligence (AI) and machine learning (ML) in the fields of radiation therapy, medical diagnostics, and occupational health and safety. Among other topics, symposium participants discussed the importance of data for AI readiness, multimodal modeling, digital twins, uncertainty quantification and trustworthiness, and bias and ethics as it applies to each of these fields.

Given the rapid advances and the regular appearance of powerful new applications in the fields of AI and ML, the symposium was particularly timely. Most likely, no area of science will be untouched by developments in AI and ML over the next few years, and this is certainly true for radiation therapy, medical diagnostics, and occupational health and safety. While these three fields are distinct and have unique ways in which AI and ML may be applied, the common theme of radiation sciences and health effects means that considering the fields jointly can be quite valuable, and the symposium was designed both to discuss specific applications for each field and to identify commonalities and themes among the fields. Each field is at a different stage in applying AI and ML models, and one goal of the symposium was to act as a platform to share ideas and methods between the fields.

The sponsors of the Nuclear and Radiation Studies Board and this symposium include the Office of Environment, Health, Safety, and Security and the Office of Environmental Management at the U.S. Department of Energy; the U.S. Nuclear Regulatory Commission; the Gordon and Betty Moore Foundation; the Richard M. Lounsbery Foundation; the American College of Radiology; and the National Academy of Sciences' Thomas Lincoln Casey Fund. The statement of task for the symposium is given in Box 1-1.

BOX 1-1
Statement of Task

An ad hoc planning committee of the National Academies of Sciences, Engineering, and Medicine will organize a symposium to discuss current and future applications of artificial intelligence (AI) and machine learning (ML) in radiation therapy, medical diagnostics, and radiation occupation safety. Specifically, the symposium will include:

Conversations led by thought leaders from a few select fields outside of medical and occupational safety (e.g., computation, transportation, legal, military, etc.) to foster community connections.

Symposium participants will then discuss:

The critical role of human decision making in the context of AI/ML (e.g., when do algorithms advise, extend, or supplant professional medical decisions).

Future directions and opportunities in AI/ML methods and technology to advance the fields of radiation therapy, medical diagnostics, and radiation occupational health and safety.

- Where has each subfield been focusing efforts in AI/ML?
- What leading/guiding practices are currently being used?
- Where would the field like to go?
- What is the biggest hurdle being faced by each subfield?

The key challenges in data quality control with respect to reproducibility, generalization of datasets, data/model drift, and trustworthiness of results with respect to each subfield of radiation therapy, medical diagnostics, and radiation occupational safety. This discussion will also include intentionality of data collection, detector development, and dataset management for future AI/ML end algorithm applications and considered trustworthiness.

Current methodologies used when implementing AI/ML techniques for each subfield and discussions on ways to learn from other fields and identify key challenges and gaps in each subfield.

Possible ethical implications of AI/ML applications in each subfield and a community discussion on possible future directions to maximize benefits and minimize negative implications.

Tailored breakout sessions to cover specific applications of AI/ML including but not limited to: creating predictive models for estimating dose in occupational environments exposed to radiation, dose distribution models for treatment planning, predictive AI/ML techniques in cancer diagnosis and treatment, integration of AI/ML into accurate and ethical human decision making, AI/ML uses to address educational and workforce shortages of radiation medical professionals, and thresholds of uncertainty acceptable for use of AI/ML in radiation applications.

The symposium presentations and discussions will be summarized in a National Academies proceedings.

ORGANIZATION OF THE PROCEEDINGS

This Proceedings of a Symposium summarizes the presentations and discussions that occurred at the Gilbert W. Beebe symposium and is not intended to provide a comprehensive and detailed account of the information shared during the symposium. The information summarized here reflects the knowledge and opinions of individual symposium participants and should not be seen as a consensus of the symposium participants, the planning committee, or the National Academies of Sciences, Engineering, and Medicine. The structure approximately mirrors the agenda of the symposium (see Appendix A), although the symposium's second day had multiple sessions occurring simultaneously, which have been arranged to best follow the narrative of the proceedings. Additionally, summaries of presentations may appear in a different order than the order in which the presentations themselves were given, for narrative flow. The remainder of this proceedings comprises eight additional chapters.

Chapter 2 offers some broader information on AI and how it is being applied in various areas. This chapter primarily addresses the line in the statement of task on "Conversations led by thought leaders from a few select fields outside of medical and occupational safety to foster community connections". It sets the stage for numerous topics discussed throughout the symposium but also touching upon points in the Statement of Task such as: principles for responsible AI development, human decision making in AI, ethical considerations, workforce development, and acceptable uncertainty levels for AI model outputs.

Chapter 3 offers a discussion of how AI and ML are being used in the three fields that were the focus of the symposium: radiation therapy, medical diagnostics, and occupational health and safety. This session primarily covers the lines in the statement of task: "Current methodologies used when implementing AI/ML techniques for each subfield and discussions on ways to learn from other fields and identify key challenges and gaps in each subfield" and "Future directions and opportunities in AI/ML methods and technology to advance the fields of radiation therapy, medical diagnostics, and radiation occupational health and safety." However, other themes such as: critical role of human decision-making, ethics, workforce development are addressed.

Chapter 4 discusses various data issues relevant to AI and ML; this is a key subject because AI models rely on large datasets for their training, addressing the line "intentionality of data collection, detector development, and data set management for future AI/ML end algorithm applications." Additional topics discussed as they relate to the statement of task include: workforce development, human decision making, and education/training.

The remaining chapters summarize focused topics identified by committee addressing issues in the Statement of Task's final subtask.

Chapter 5 focuses on a particular type of AI model—digital twins—that has potential for medicine and public health applications. This covers predictive modeling, dose distribution models, and predictive AI/ML techniques in cancer diagnosis and treatment from the statement of task.

Chapter 6 focuses on examples of how AI is being applied in various radiation-related areas but with a focus on multimodal applications of AI. This addresses predictive modeling, human decision making, and begins to address uncertainty and trustworthiness of models.

Chapter 7 discusses bias, ethics, and regulatory topics that have relevance to applications of AI to the fields of radiation therapy, medical diagnostics, and occupational health and safety. This session also cover federal regulations and discusses bias in AI models.

Chapter 8 covers topics that are concerned with trustworthiness, and transparency in AI. There are presentations and discussions also addressing uncertainty quantification and risk mitigation.

Finally, Chapter 9 offers final remarks. The themes of human decision making, ethics, considerations of model uncertainty, education, and workforce development are interwoven throughout presentations and discussions.

2
Insights from the Artificial Intelligence Field

The first panel, chaired by Leo Chiang, senior research and development fellow of the Dow Chemical Company, and Shaheen Dewji, assistant professor in the Nuclear and Radiological Engineering and Medical Physics Program at the Georgia Institute of Technology, set the stage for the rest of the meeting by offering insights from artificial intelligence (AI) developers, users, and government regulators on balancing the benefits of rapid AI innovation with the risks, led by thought leaders to foster community connections. The topics included principles for responsible AI development, human decision making in AI, ethical considerations, and acceptable uncertainty levels for AI model outputs.

TRANSFORMATIONAL AI OPPORTUNITIES IN HEALTHCARE

David C. Rhew, global chief medical officer and vice president of healthcare for Microsoft, began by offering several examples of how AI is already being used in healthcare and then sketching what will be important in the future if AI is to assume a major role in clinical care. His presentation had four main components: an examination of how to leverage technological innovation to enable the use of AI in healthcare, how to ensure trust related to AI in healthcare, how to democratize AI, and how to develop a workforce that can take advantage of AI's potential for use in healthcare.

Rhew began by saying that while most people associate AI in healthcare with improving operational efficiencies and enhancing the overall care experience, the technology's greatest impact will likely come from enabling entirely new capabilities, particularly in making healthcare more proactive than reactive. The concept of preventing illness before it occurs has existed for decades, but healthcare practitioners have historically been limited to a small set of tools including education, symptom awareness training, vaccination programs, and basic screening initiatives. AI now offers a powerful new addition to this tool kit, providing the potential to screen large populations and identify at-risk individuals before they become symptomatic and enabling targeted interventions that could dramatically improve health outcomes.

Rhew stated that the current healthcare system requires individuals to seek clinical care actively, but many people have minimal contact with healthcare providers until they experience serious issues such as heart attacks, strokes, or advanced cancers that can no longer be ignored. This population represents exactly the group that healthcare systems hope to reach earlier in the disease process, and AI holds tremendous promise for identifying and engaging these individuals before they reach crisis points.

One of the most compelling examples, in Rhew's opinion, of AI's transformative potential lies in routine eye examinations. Traditionally, retinal images captured during eye exams remained stored on imaging equipment with little additional analysis beyond the immediate examination. However, AI can now analyze these retinal images to screen for multiple conditions including diabetic retinopathy, cardiovascular disease, hypertension, chronic kidney disease, ophthalmologic conditions, and even neurovascular disorders.

This advancement has been made possible by optical coherence tomography (OCT), which provides three-dimensional images at submicron resolution compared to the two-dimensional surface images produced by traditional fundoscopy. OCT enables identification of arterioles, nerves, and surrounding retinal structures, essentially providing magnetic resonance imaging–level detail at a fraction of the cost and with much greater accessibility. While OCT technology itself is not new, recent innovations have automated the data acquisition process, reducing examination time from 20 minutes with a clinician to just 2 minutes without clinical supervision, making it practical for routine screening.

Rhew provided the example that Stanford Medical School has implemented this approach in satellite clinics, where patients receive routine OCT examinations alongside standard vital sign measurements. The results have been dramatic; Healthcare Effectiveness Data and Information Set (HEDIS) scores improved from 20–40 percent to more than 80–90 percent in participating clinics, while overall system HEDIS scores have increased substantially. The technology also generates revenue through established Current Procedural Terminology codes.

Beyond diabetic retinopathy detection, OCT serves as a portal into systemic health conditions throughout the body. Research published in *Nature Communications* demonstrated that chronic kidney disease causes thinning of choroidal and retinal membranes in the eye, while kidney transplantation restores choroidal membrane thickness but not retinal membrane thickness (Farrah et al., 2023). This reveals that membrane thickness detected by OCT serves as a dynamic indicator of glomerular function, illustrating how systemic diseases affect blood vessels and membranes uniformly throughout the body.

Current research is exploring connections between ocular and neurovascular conditions including Alzheimer's disease, multiple sclerosis, and Parkinson's disease. The eye may ultimately serve as a comprehensive screening and monitoring platform for numerous systemic conditions, representing a paradigm shift toward holistic health assessment through a single accessible examination.

Rhew then discussed how AI applications in electronic health record (EHR) analysis may reveal gaps in clinical care and missed diagnoses. While ideal medical practice would involve evidence-based care without any gaps, reality demonstrates wide variability in clinical performance. AI analysis of medical records could close this gap and potentially identify patients with diseases that were missed during clinical encounters.

An AI platform developed by Pangaea Data analyzed medical records and identified 296 percent more lung cancer patients than had International Classification of Diseases codes for lung cancer, 179 percent more patients with ovarian cancer, and 71 percent more patients with lupus nephritis. Among cancer patients specifically, AI analysis revealed numerous cases where appropriate biomarker testing was not performed, and when testing was completed, results were not concordant with prescribed treatments; this suggests that diagnostic tests were ordered but not acted upon. He said, the frequency of such clinical oversights is surprisingly high and represents a significant opportunity for improvement.

Rhew noted that he is seeing some programs across the country now use AI to analyze medical records and identify care gaps, particularly focusing on patients who are eligible for specific treatments but are not receiving appropriate care. He believes this application has substantial implications for clinical trial enrollment and overall patient management, ensuring that eligible patients receive optimal care and are considered for relevant research opportunities.

Another frontier in AI-powered healthcare applications that Rhew mentioned was voice analysis. While healthcare providers have long used dictation and transcription services for medical documentation, and ambient voice technologies now convert clinician–patient conversations into medical records, the capture of voice data opens new possibilities for AI analysis of both patient and clinician speech patterns.

Existing AI programs can analyze voices to detect depression, stress, and anxiety, for example, with validation against established screening tools. This capability eliminates the need for patients to complete traditional survey instruments, providing real-time assessment of mental and emotional states during clinical encounters. These tools can identify and quantify depression and anxiety levels, assist in clinical trial candidate identification, and monitor clinician burnout, representing a significant expansion of diagnostic capabilities without additional patient burden.

Rhew noted, disease identification through AI represents only the first step in a three-phase approach to population health improvement. The subsequent phases involve risk stratification, triage, and capacity building (the overall improvement in the organization's ability to produce, perform, or deploy), followed by education, engagement, and activation. These latter phases often present the greatest barriers, particularly in underserved and rural communities, but AI can contribute significantly to each component.

Identifying large numbers of individuals with specific conditions and treatment needs, especially in underserved areas, can overwhelm already stressed healthcare systems, increasing wait times and reducing timely care delivery. Risk stratification and triage may become essential for prioritizing the highest-risk patients, while capacity building can help ensure the system can accommodate increased demand. Many patients of specialists and primary care physicians already face extended wait times, making capacity optimization crucial.

Rhew offered one example of how AI could help with this. AI-powered pre-screening could identify higher-risk patients requiring specialist care while directing other cases to optometrists, enabling ophthalmologists to practice at higher complexity levels while optimizing overall system efficiency. Optometrists represent one of the fastest-growing healthcare professions, making this approach particularly viable for expanding access to eye care (Tang, 2025).

The Alliance for Healthcare from the Eye exemplifies this comprehensive approach by involving multiple government agencies, healthcare systems, and payers in an initiative to screen the entire U.S. population for advanced-stage chronic disease using OCT-based screening methods deployed in Stanford-associated clinics nationwide. This program aims to demonstrate the feasibility of population-wide AI-powered health screening.

Patient engagement represents the final component of population health improvement. Rhew noted that simply identifying diseases and building capacity does not guarantee patient participation in care. Educating about risks and treatment options, enhancing healthcare system engagement, and addressing social determinants of health all contribute to successful population health programs, he said. No single organization can address all these components effectively, highlighting the importance of partnerships among organizations specializing in different aspects of the care continuum.

Rhew said that these partnerships include organizations capable of identifying individuals through imaging, blood biomarkers, wearable devices, and EHR analysis, as well as entities that can perform risk stratification and capacity building. Digital health companies provide education, behavioral nudging, and ongoing support through chatbots and other AI-powered mechanisms. He stated that successful implementation requires coordinated integration of these diverse capabilities rather than isolated problem-solving approaches.

Rhew then discussed the Trustworthy and Responsible AI Network, established in March 2024 as a consortium spanning the United States and Europe, which focuses on key principles of responsible AI including transparency, explainability, validation, and bias assessment. The consortium emphasizes efficient processes for establishing responsible AI within institutions while optimizing time, resources, and costs.

He outlined three primary goals that guide efficient operationalization of responsible AI. First, technology could facilitate implementation rather than relying solely on manual processes such as individual model reviews in meetings. Second, collaboration among health systems enables shared learning at the model level. Third, ensuring that no systems are left behind addresses resource disparities that might prevent some organizations from participating in AI advancement.

The consortium identified four essential components for institutional AI leadership. First, registration involves identifying all AI systems currently operating within an organization, which involves defining what constitutes "AI" and focusing specifically on clinical AI applications. The fundamental principle that improvement involves measurement and measurement warrants tracking makes AI registration important for responsible implementation using standardized "model cards."

Second, testing encompasses both pre- and post-deployment evaluation of AI systems on local datasets. Rhew mentioned that, previously, organizations often assumed that externally developed models had undergone sufficient testing and could be trusted for local applications. However, rapid AI advancement has highlighted the importance of local testing and ongoing monitoring to ensure reasonable performance on institutional datasets.

Third, bias assessment involves evaluating AI systems for discriminatory outcomes and implementing mitigation measures. Monitoring extends beyond model performance to include outcome assessment, with particular attention to subpopulation performance to detect bias in model results. Fourth, governance necessitates establishing scalable processes for responsible AI oversight to ensure systematic management of AI implementations across the organization.

Rhew discussed how various technologies support these four areas, may include tools for identifying hallucinations in large language models (LLMs), bias assessment capabilities, and quality assurance mechanisms (Bird, 2024). However, technology alone is insufficient; examining outcomes introduces implementation variables that significantly impact performance.

The initial deployment of EHRs illustrates the importance of implementation factors. Rhew said that despite assumptions that superior user interfaces would produce better outcomes, research demonstrated similar performance across different EHR systems, with the greatest variability occurring within the same EHR due to implementation differences. He stated that this emphasizes the importance of understanding not only AI model outcomes but also implementation details including who receives outputs, timing of delivery, format of presentation, and subsequent actions taken.

Democratizing healthcare AI involves enabling rural and resource-limited hospitals to access AI advances comparable to those of academic and urban medical centers. Most organizations currently attempt to build proprietary models, essentially "reinventing the wheel," despite the difficulty of developing models that incorporate multiple data modalities.

Healthcare AI models commonly utilize EHR data, imaging data, and genomics data. Multimodal models combining two or more of these data types provide more comprehensive patient assessments and enable three distinct capabilities: Risk categorization assigns patients to low-, medium-, or high-risk groups. Cohort matching places patients into groups similar to entire databases, enabling outcome predictions for patient populations without specific clinical trial data through longitudinal database analysis. Predictive modeling forecasts specific patient outcomes based on comprehensive data integration.

Rhew noted that "adapted multimodal AI models"—those that can process both images and text—could serve multiple organizations without requiring individual development efforts. Many AI tasks are common across organizations and models. He noted that in imaging applications, structure identification represents a fundamental requirement for all foundation models, involving boundary detection that every group should implement. Rather than each group developing these basic capabilities independently, models can be fine-tuned to adapt pre-trained foundation models to specific datasets and questions, such as cancer subtype analysis. This approach LLMs as general reasoning engines, enabling users to query foundation models, perform tasks, and generate results.

This embedded approach—where AI capabilities are integrated directly into existing clinical workflows and imaging systems—involving model adaptation to specific datasets and questions with general reasoning capabilities, offers significant advantages over traditional single-model applications to various datasets. Reduced hallucination susceptibility represents a key benefit, leading to widespread adoption of this approach across various AI applications.

Recent work published in *Nature* describes a whole-slide foundation model trained on Providence's collection of 1.3 billion pathology image tiles from 171,000 whole slides representing more than 30,000 patients from 28 cancer centers across 31 major tissue types (Xu et al., 2024). This foundation model enables gene mutation prediction and cancer subtyping and has been made open source to accelerate development, following a trend toward open-source foundation model availability.

Rhew commented that rural hospitals would have to address fundamental infrastructure needs before deploying advanced technologies such as AI. For example, he continued, affordable broadband access represents a primary requirement and is supported by significant national initiatives. Cloud access with integrated cybersecurity represents another essential component, and one that Microsoft is hoping to address through their Cybersecurity Program for rural hospitals.

Rhew described efforts to make Rural Health AI Lab consortia focuses on AI applications specifically relevant to rural hospitals, particularly cybersecurity applications and insurance claim denial assistance. More than 550 rural hospitals participate in these efforts, demonstrating growing recognition of the benefits of a trustworthy, responsible AI network.

He went on to explain that successful network creation extends beyond technology to collaborative approaches, particularly hub-and-spoke models where high-resource settings partner with low-resource settings to share technologies, best practices, and costs. Data sharing represents only one component; ensuring that model developers feel confident about intellectual property protection is equally important.

Rhew noted that federated learning strategies may be developed that maintain data privacy, but some model developers avoid participation due to model exposure requirements, as models represent highly sensitive intellectual property. Security enclaves where models are maintained and used for data analysis, combined with data-in-use encryption, ensure protection of both models and data during analysis.

Rhew stated that he believes healthcare AI workforce development could address a transition similar to that of previous technological revolutions, in which certain jobs become obsolete while others emerge. This transition uniquely affects knowledge workers, including clinicians, lawyers, and engineers, rather than primarily impacting those in manual labor roles.

To address this, Rhew provided the example of how other companies are thinking about next-generation healthcare jobs to include AI model engineers, prompt engineers, AI data scientists, AI developers, AI governance specialists, and Machine Translation Post-Editors. According to McKinsey predictions, these translators who interpret and adapt AI for businesses and users will experience the greatest demand, representing a critical workforce development consideration (Singla, 2025).

Rhew highlighted how Microsoft is working on a three-step program in collaboration with multiple sites nationwide to address workforce transition needs: Education provides fundamental AI knowledge and an understanding of related ethical considerations. Skills development enables effective use of tools such as prompt engineering and AI collaboration techniques. Job specification defines new role requirements and responsibilities.

Rhew explained that AI transformation affects diverse roles including call center agents, legal clerks, and numerous other positions. Specifying new job requirements and building programs that provide both certification and employment opportunities includes collaboration between academia and industry. This comprehensive approach ensures that workforce development aligns with technological advancement while providing meaningful career pathways for affected workers.

The integration of AI into healthcare represents a fundamental shift from reactive to proactive care delivery, with applications spanning from routine screening to complex population health management. Rhew stated that he believes success requires coordinated implementation of technological capabilities, responsible governance frameworks, and comprehensive workforce development to ensure that AI's transformative potential benefits all healthcare stakeholders while maintaining safety, equity, and effectiveness standards.

PROMOTING A SAFE AND EFFECTIVE CLINICAL ENVIRONMENT FOR AI

Mike Tilkin, chief information officer and executive vice president for technology at the American College of Radiology (ACR), spoke about the journey to safe and effective AI adoption, with a focus on what the ACR has been doing to reach that point.

Tilkin began by providing background on ACR, an organization more than a century old with approximately 40,000 members including radiologists and radiation oncologists. The group's primary mission is "to serve patients and society by empowering [its] members to advance the practice, science, and professions of radiological care." In 2017, the board decided to "really lean into" the emerging area of AI and data science, establishing as a basic tenet that "we wanted to advance data science as core to clinically relevant, safe, and effective radiologic care." Recognizing that AI and data science would become central components of medicine and radiology, the organization has engaged "professionals and volunteers and really quite a bit of machinery of the ACR" in contemplating the AI revolution.

From the provider perspective, Tilkin presented data from a 2024 AI survey conducted by ACR's Data Science Institute. Nearly 1,000 ACR members responded, with 86 percent reporting they were using AI in some part of their practice—a dramatic increase from only 58 percent in 2022. When asked about their motivations for using AI, radiologists most commonly cited desires to automate monotonous tasks, save time, and enhance accuracy or precision. "Clearly there is an appetite in the radiology community for this technology," Tilkin noted.

The attitude toward AI in the radiology community has evolved significantly over the past decade. In 2017, AI-related questions were typically "What is this AI?" and "What is it going to do for me?" Today, after years of hearing about AI's revolutionary potential, the questions have shifted to "Why isn't it helping me do my work better?" Tilkin said, this change reflects the community's strong interest in realizing the promised benefits of AI technology.

However, significant concerns persist. The 2024 survey identified the two greatest AI-related concerns as issues with accuracy and errors and the potential for liability. These concerns highlight the importance of AI solutions that ensure accuracy and compliance with safety protocols, provide risk mitigation strategies for adopting practices, and highlight trustworthy products that mitigate medico-legal liability. According to the survey, most in the radiology community trust AI moderately or somewhat.

The survey results revealed mixed success in meeting expectations. Three-quarters of respondents said AI met or exceeded their expectations on ease of use, but half reported it failed to meet expectations on return on investment and supporting clinical decision making. Specifically, only 42 percent agreed that "I find most AI outputs to be clinically meaningful," and just 18 percent agreed that "AI outputs frequently modify my clinical decision making." While much work remains, Tilkin noted that the technology is still very new, and current solutions are early iterations.

Transitioning to marketplace dynamics, Tilkin drew on concepts from Everett M. Rogers's classic 1962 book *Diffusion of Innovations*. When new technology is introduced, early adopters tend to be risk takers willing to "wade through a problematic technology and try and realize the benefit." The next user group is more data-driven, wanting to see proven solutions and requiring vendors to demonstrate value clearly. Finally, late adopters are skeptics with low tolerance for failure who need solid infrastructure and platforms that ensure success, because "they are just not going to tolerate subpar solutions."

Tilkin also referenced the Gartner Hype Cycle, which describes how expectations for new technologies cycle through early development, a peak of inflated expectation, a trough of disillusionment, and finally realistic expectations as technology matures (Gartner, 2025). For AI in radiology, the peak of inflated expectation occurred around 2017 after Nobel Prize winner Geoff Hinton predicted that AI would make radiologists obsolete within 5 years (Byju, 2024). Today, AI in radiology is in the maturity phase, with numerous market products and clearer expectations emerging.

The ACR has been working for years to identify gaps in this technology while developing standards and interoperability. "For this market to mature," Tilkin explained, "there are going to have to be sufficient standards that the vendors can build mature workflow solutions." Simultaneously, the field is working with regulators to help understand testing requirements for this new technology while addressing ongoing concerns about ethics and bias in AI radiology applications.

The evolution of the field is evident in annual summits held by ACR with the Society for Imaging Informatics in Medicine. In 2018, their "conversations were very much general: How do we think about the economics of AI? How do we think about getting data?" Recent summits have focused on implementation questions, such as demonstrating return on investment to stakeholders and ensuring appropriate testing in production environments.

ACR has also worked extensively on developing use cases and specifications to "provide an anchor for what these algorithms were doing, how to think about what success looks like, and how to think about how they are triggered." While AI models are covering more clinical areas, significant gaps remain. Currently, about 351 AI software and medical device solutions have Food and Drug Administration (FDA) approval and are market-available, but "we're still fairly early in providing solutions that range across the spectrum," Tilkin said.

Tilkin then discussed workforce training and how it has become an ACR focus in recent years. He explained, "At the very least, we need everybody to be conversant, be a good consumer, understand the basics of the technology" while also developing groups with increasingly sophisticated AI understanding up to those capable of creating AI products. Various tools foster engagement and literacy, including the ACR AI-LAB, a workbench allowing hands-on technology engagement and model creation for educational purposes.

Data are crucial for AI development, prompting several radiological data collection efforts. Examples include updating the National Lung Screening Trial with AI-appropriate data as well as updating the Medical Imaging and Data Resource Center, operated under ACR auspices with the National Institute of Biomedical Imaging and Bioengineering and others, with COVID-19–related data.

ACR has emphasized federated learning, believing it is "critical that we move the analysis to where the data [are]." The organization has undertaken numerous projects focusing on training models in institutions by moving models to institutions for local data training and testing. Federated learning enables model training across multiple sites while keeping data local, although ensuring proper data curation remains critical.

Currently, ACR works with approximately 40,000 nationwide facilities, requiring software creation and deployment to communicate with local systems and collect data. Tools called TRIAD and ACR Connect are used to engage with local systems and participate in large data projects. ACR also collaborates with regulators, payers, and industry on policy topics like AI oversight in radiology and works with FDA on real-world testing of approved and marketed algorithms to verify that performance characteristics meet expectations.

Moving to a discussion of scaling AI adoption, Tilkin described several ACR efforts to increase effective AI use in radiology clinics, particularly targeting late adopters and those awaiting better infrastructure.

AI Central—a free ACR resource cataloging market-available AI products for radiology use—represents a key initiative. The concept involves collecting all platform, product, and manufacturer details in one location. Its necessity "speaks to the fact that this is a tough market to penetrate if you're sitting on the outside looking in," Tilkin explained.

AI Central allows users to examine FDA-approved products for specific uses. One clear outcome is that most current market products serve triage or operational functions rather than detection and diagnosis, because FDA approval bars are much higher for the latter. However, available data show increasing numbers of FDA-approved products entering the market over time.

ACR promotes transparency regarding AI model contents in its database. Details provided about each product include training data characteristics and performance statistics. ACR encourages vendors to make these data public so consumers better understand their purchases. "We think it is a critically important part of the puzzle," Tilkin noted.

Monitoring real-world product performance is another vital marketplace aspect. At the end of 2024, ACR launched the Assess-AI registry to monitor AI results. The registry collects AI outputs from vendors and compares them with "ground truth" from radiology reports to determine agreement frequency between AI results and radiologist-generated results. Extensive contextual information is collected, with de-identified data loaded into the registry for analysis.

The registry provides concordance rates indicating how well particular model results agree with radiologists' results, analyzed by individual facilities and demographic features like age and sex. Individual facility concordance rates can be compared with national averages and examined longitudinally to track performance improvements or deterioration over time. The most important signal, Tilkin suggested, can be simply observing performance changes over time, indicating that something may need attention.

A related program is ARCH-AI (ACR Recognized Center for Healthcare-AI), described as the "first national AI quality assurance program for radiology facilities." Its base function offers recognition for good AI technology work through ARCH-AI designation. Beyond that, "increasing levels of formality" exist, including formal accreditation programs and specific designations like the Diagnostic Imaging Center of Excellence designation. The accreditation program builds on the recognition program by adding white papers, practice parameters, and technical standards; Tilkin noted that he and colleagues had published a process description article (see Larson et al., 2025).

As discussed by Tilkin, the accreditation process evaluates institutions across four key areas. First, governance involves having institutions establish formal programs that create policies for model evaluation, acceptance, monitoring, and retirement. These institutions should maintain inventories of all clinically deployed models and require mandatory cybersecurity and compliance reviews before any deployment. Second, model selection follows predetermined, formal processes where each AI model's intended purpose is clearly documented. Third, acceptance testing involves formal, documented procedures along with proper training for all clinicians and staff who will use the models. Finally, institutions demonstrate effective monitoring practices.

Tilkin described a typical deployment pathway starting with nonclinical setting deployment, usually on retrospective data, followed by "shadow deployment" in production settings where models are not used clinically yet but performance can be monitored. Next comes limited deployment for assessing model performance before full rollout. The fourth factor is monitoring, specifically local monitoring and registry participation.

Finally, he noted that institutions developing AI applications locally cannot take shortcuts. He said that just as institutions call for rigorous vendor development, they should demand the same rigor of themselves, including using trained and trusted personnel and following standard procedures.

Tilkin finished by examining LLMs, vision language models, and generative AI. He highlighted the dramatic field advancement since neural networks of a decade ago. At that time, the largest neural networks had tens of millions of trainable parameters, while in 2024 OpenAI's Generative Pretrained Transformer 4 (GPT-4) had more than 1 trillion trainable parameters.

This growth accompanied dramatic power increases. "Back in 2018 when we were all excited about cat and dog recognizers, I put an image of my dog into a recognizer that said, yes, this is a dog," he recalled. Better models would identify breeds, but when he provided the full image instead of a cropped version, they struggled significantly. The full image showed his dog in front of a ripped sofa and cushion filling, apparently pulled out by the dog, and neural networks could not interpret the filling—one thought it might be popcorn.

However, when Tilkin showed the same picture to ChatGPT, released in November 2022, it knew exactly what was depicted. It recognized the dog and the sofa (although the latter was misidentified as a chair); correctly identified the cushion filling; and even surmised the dog might be the culprit, noting a "guilty or sheepish" look on the dog's face. This represented incredible capability advancement in just 4 years.

Tilkin offered examples of exercises used in his laboratory to build comfort with and demonstrate usage of AI. In one case, an LLM made a radiology report user-friendly, while in another, the model extracted quantitative characteristics from reports (such as kidney length and gallstone numbers) and created tables. The real purpose was building AI familiarity and capability understanding.

Tilkin next talked about how ACR also focuses on testing various AI models, leading to the creation of the Healthcare AI Challenge consortium for AI model validation and monitoring. The consortium includes ACR's Data Science Institute along with Mass General Brigham, Emory Healthcare, University of Wisconsin–Madison School of Medicine and Public Health, and UW (University of Washington) Medicine. The consortium's goal is collecting geographically and demographically diverse data, particularly embargoed data not used for AI model training; defining clinical use cases (e.g., draft report generation); and engaging geographically and institutionally diverse experts for AI agent evaluations using input data. The consortium is similar to the Large Model Systems Organization, which develops large AI models and systems, but is focused on radiology.

The Healthcare AI Challenge concept provides a forum where AI performance ratings are posted and discussed, with healthcare professionals rating various AI model performance. Information on AI model performance can then inform internal decision making at radiology institutions using or considering AI models. As an example, Tilkin showed online pages where practitioners could rate AI model performance at reading and interpreting X-rays. Ratings use a five-level scale: unacceptable, student (poor), resident (acceptable), fellow (good), and attending (outstanding). Raters do not know which AI model they are rating until after posting ratings, at which point the model is revealed. The consortium uses scores for different models to compute Elo scores for all models, similar to chess player ratings, and users can examine ratings for different AI models and leave comments to provide the consortium with feedback.

In his ending remarks, Tilkin discussed factors influencing risk–reward calculations that individuals and organizations make when deciding whether to use healthcare AI. Subjective risk attitudes play important roles, appearing at both personal and practice levels and influenced by local market conditions. The type of intended use—triage, detection, or diagnosis—is another factor, as is the clinical use case. Finally, operational safeguards—having transparency, monitoring results, and implementing best practices—can all reduce risk, or at least risk perception, making people more likely to accept new technologies.

DISCUSSION

A brief discussion followed the two panelists' presentations, with questions posted on Slido by in-person and online audience members.

Chiang presented the first question: Given the need to collect massive amounts of personal health data to train AI models, how can data collection be encouraged before it is clear how the data will be used? Rhew responded with two key aspects. First, technology can secure data and create confidence that they will not be exposed to different organizations. "Federated learning obviously has a significant role to play in this," he continued, "because you are not releasing control of the data to another entity, and it allows you to be able to put your own safeguards in place." When institutions send data externally, they rely on other organizations for security, potentially leaving them liable for breaches.

Tilkin added that even with good data protection, model developers may hesitate to share their datasets or models because running models on external datasets can reveal model details. "This is a problem if you are trying to accelerate the amount of collaboration," Tilkin said. "This is why the privacy-preserving environments are so essential."

Rhew explained that the second aspect involves educating patients and consumers about data use. Rhew emphasized transparency: "I think it is extremely important that we address the issue of patients feeling comfortable with how we're managing [the data] and really being transparent in that process."

Tilkin agreed, adding that multimodal models complicate matters since multiple people and institutions handle different data types. As genomics and other clinical data are added, he said that "at some point you do have the need for a federation, if nothing else just to deal with the challenges, even for centrally collected data." He said, the solution is developing methods to leave data in controlled environments and bring analysis to the data rather than moving data around.

Building on that discussion, Dewji asked whether data collections should have minimal quality standards. Tilkin explained that minimal standards serve two purposes: reducing the burden of making data available (since curation is difficult and costly) and better mirroring production data. He added, "We collect data, we polish [them] up, [they look] really good, we then work with [them], and then your mileage varies when you're actually in a clinical environment."

Regarding whether AI healthcare models have a prerequisite of massive data collections with predefined uses, Tilkin noted the difficulty of getting institutions to open data for general investigations. Institutional review boards want to understand specific data uses before approving research. "Being able to turn on the 'data spigot' tends to be use-case specific," he said, due to required approvals. He noted that to obtain representative data including rural areas and underrepresented populations, strategies must account for legal and practical sharing restrictions.

Rhew emphasized understanding privacy/personal dataset sensitivity levels. Basic disease information is less sensitive than whole genome sequences, and he said that "we're now starting to realize that, based on level of sensitivity, we have to have higher levels of safeguards." Patient education about data uses and implications is crucial.

He continued by stating that assembling representative datasets is challenging because most data come from people entering medical facilities—that is, just a subset of the population. "If we truly want this to be representative of larger populations," he said, "we have strategies for how we acquire data outside of people coming into the system." Rhew mentioned a stalled initiative that would have given individuals access to their medical records to decide where information goes: "Ultimately, we wanted to empower consumers with their own health information so that they could make their own determinations."

Chiang then asked about overcoming difficulties in interpreting multimodal models containing data from clinical records, images, pathology reports, and genomic records. Rhew identified the current challenge as simply building these expensive models, which require massive amounts of diverse, well-curated datasets. One approach is assembling datasets collectively and making resulting models open source. This creates value since individual organizations do not have to build models themselves and can use unique datasets to train their own models off of collective ones. Rhew noted that LLMs can then handle complex interpretation tasks, making information readily accessible to end users. He explained, "Today, it is a lot of everyone building based on their own datasets and their own resources. That's not a scalable model." Instead, he said that different players can use coordinated strategies that leverage their unique capabilities: "Most organizations would love to be in a place where they can accelerate the development of their models and do it in a way that creates new valuable [intellectual property] for them."

Regarding the best way to present uncertainty in AI model outputs, Tilkin noted that current vendor solutions differ in presenting uncertainty to radiologists and end users. The strategy depends on algorithm details, but feedback loops—that "provide feedback on what the model is doing, what the confidence intervals are, [and] what the uncertainty looks like"—are important. These allow users to process information, make decisions, and provide feedback. He claimed that vendors should avoid black-box presentations and give context for model answers.

Rhew explained that the field is moving from single models handling everything toward workflows and models specific to particular scenarios. Each model excels at its task with high confidence and then communicates with the others. This approach mitigates concerns about AI hallucination or other failures. "We're starting to realize that as much as LLMs can do so many amazing things, if we just simply let one LLM try to solve all the problems, we run into a lot of issues with certain types of use cases," he said.

The next question concerned preventing data monetization by vendors. Rhew said finding the right balance is important since innovation is driven by organizations generating revenue through value creation. Transparency—making sure people know what they are signing up for—is key: "I do not think there is anything wrong with businesses thriving in the pursuit of something that's very beneficial for individuals if everyone is aware of it," he said.

Tilkin agreed about transparency's importance in ensuring people understand what data are used and how. Increasingly, data contributors want to see results from their data. "So the more you can just provide transparency on what data [are] being used, [and] in what context, I think the better off we'll be," he continued.

The final question addressed balancing healthcare AI benefits with possibilities that patients are stigmatized by AI detecting issues, like depression, that may not have been detected previously. Rhew noted the medical community underdiagnoses for various reasons: "We're oftentimes too busy. We do not ask the right questions. The patients do not share the information. And because of that underdiagnosis, when bad things happen, we always wonder, 'I wish we would have been able to have identified that.'" AI is valuable for uncovering undiagnosed conditions. However, he continued, when AI makes discoveries, "there will, in some cases, be a conversation that needs to occur, and it needs to be done with sensitivity." AI uncovers problems rather than solving them; Rhew stated that clinicians should communicate with empathy, compassion, and contextual understanding.

With patients increasingly accessing laboratory results, people might discover conditions before clinicians can discuss them. Rhew noted that the AI issue is "just another example of how we need to smooth out these rollouts and processes so that when sensitive information is identified, there is always a clinician there to be able to make that communication as seamless as possible."

Tilkin added that agents could be particularly useful, allowing clinicians to set rules about information exposure timing and location and enabling intervention when needed. As health information is collected for various purposes, information flow could become bidirectional, with AI models choosing when and how to provide information to patients. "The question ultimately is how we fold this into the workflow [of the] clinician–patient dynamic, but the potential is tremendous," Tilkin explained.

REFERENCES

Bird, S. 2024. "Announcing new tools in Azure AI to help you build more secure and trustworthy generative AI applications." Microsoft Azure Blog. https://azure.microsoft.com/en-us/blog/announcing-new-tools-in-azure-ai-to-help-you-build-more-secure-and-trustworthy-generative-ai-applications/ (accessed July 1, 2025).

Byju, A. 2024. The "Godfather of AI" predicted I wouldn't have a job. He was wrong. *New Republic*, October 25. https://newrepublic.com/article/187203/ai-radiology-geoffrey-hinton-nobel-prediction.

Farrah, T. E., D. Pugh, F. A. Chapman, E. Godden, C. Balmforth, G. Oniscu, D. Webb, B. Dhillon, J. Dear, M. Bailey, P. Gallacher, and N. Dhaun. 2023. Choroidal and retinal thinning in chronic kidney disease independently associate with eGFR decline and are modifiable with treatment. *Nature Communications* 14:7720.

Gartner. 2025. *Gartner Hype Cycle*. https://www.gartner.com/en/research/methodologies/gartner-hype-cycle.

Larson, D. B., M. Bhargavan-Chatfield, M. Tilkin, L. Coombs, and C. Wald. 2025. The road map for ACR practice accreditation for radiology artificial intelligence. *Journal of the American College of Radiology* 22(5):586–592.

Rogers, E. M. 1962. *Diffusion of innovations*. New York: The Free Press of Glencoe.

Singla, A., A. Sukharevsky, L. Lee, M. Chui, and B. Hall. March 2025. "The State of AI: Global Survey, McKinsey." https://www.mckinsey.com/capabilities/quantumblack/our-insights/the-state-of-ai#.

Tang, L. 2025. Optometrists in the US—Market Research Report (2015–2030). IBISWorld, February 2025. https://www.ibisworld.com/united-states/industry/optometrists/1560.

Xu, H., N. Usuyama, J. Bagga, S. Zhang, R. Rao, T. Naumann, C. Wong, Z. Gero, J. González, Y. Gu, Y. Xu, M. Wei, W. Wang, S. Ma, F. Wei, J. Yang, C. Li, J. Gao, J. Rosemon, T. Bower, S. Lee, R. Weerasinghe, B. J. Wright, A. Robicsek, B. Piening, C. Bifulco, S. Wang, and H. Poon. 2024. A whole-slide foundation model for digital pathology from real-world data. *Nature* 630(8015):181–188.

3
The Potential for Use of Artificial Intelligence in Radiation Health Fields

The state of the art in using artificial intelligence (AI) in radiation health was the main topic of three separate panels at the symposium. The panels were focused on the use of AI in three different areas: medical diagnostics, radiation therapy and oncology, and radiation occupational health and future directions and opportunities in AI and machine learning (ML) methods and technology to advance each of those fields. Although these three areas differ in the specific ways that AI is used and the degree to which AI applications have been applied, common themes did emerge among the areas.

MEDICAL DIAGNOSTICS

The panel on the use of AI in medical diagnostics was chaired by Caroline Chung, vice president and chief data and analytics officer, co-director of the Institute for Data Science and Oncology, and professor in radiation oncology and diagnostic imaging at MD Anderson Cancer Center in Houston.

Uses of AI in Imaging

Jayashree Kalpathy-Cramer, endowed chair in ophthalmic data science and founding chief of the Division of Artificial Medical Intelligence in the Department of Ophthalmology at the University of Colorado School of Medicine, provided an overview of how AI is transforming medical imaging. She emphasized that AI and ML are used throughout the entire patient journey, from accelerating image acquisition and reconstruction to improving diagnosis and treatment monitoring. While radiology has been at the forefront of AI adoption in healthcare, she noted a significant gulf between theoretical capabilities and clinical implementation.

Despite tremendous progress in foundation models, large language models, and vision models, relatively little has been translated to clinical practice. "There are many different reasons why that might be," she said, "but I'm hoping that, as a community, we figure out how to translate things and move them from what's possible to what we really like to see."

Kalpathy-Cramer discussed how deep learning has made substantial advances in computed tomography (CT) image reconstruction, with many algorithms now commercially available and deployed. She noted that these AI reconstructions enable 30–71 percent reduction in necessary CT doses compared to hybrid iterative reconstruction, while maintaining image quality (Koetzier et al., 2023). Deep learning methods for metal artifact reduction also appear to remove artifacts more accurately than current state-of-the-art approaches.

Various approaches exist for converting low-dose scans to high-quality images, including direct conversion methods and hybrid approaches that combine deep learning with traditional reconstruction techniques. These hybrid methods might use deep learning to improve scan quality, apply traditional reconstruction methods, and then employ additional deep learning to enhance image resolution.

Extensive AI development has occurred over the past 5–10 years and is now entering routine clinical use in segmentation—that is, the delineation of object boundaries in images. This technology is particularly valuable for radiation therapy planning in oncology and radiation oncology for quantifying tumor burden and contouring tumors and organs at risk during radiation. AI segmentation not only makes radiologists' jobs easier but also potentially reduces variability and improves conformity (Elhalawani et al., 2019; Ng et al., 2018).

A study involving Kalpathy-Cramer's team demonstrated that an AI model performed as well as five expert radiologists in segmenting CT images of adrenal glands (Robinson-Weiss et al., 2023). Significant work has also been done on AI-based brain tumor segmentation (Beers et al., 2021; Chang et al., 2019; Peng et al., 2022), with the number of available algorithms greatly increasing. AI can also track temporal changes in tumor configuration—something difficult with standard clinical assessments that focus on overall volume rather than precise morphology.

AI tools enable comprehensive body analysis from images taken for specific purposes, making opportunistic screening possible. By segmenting all body components—organs, bones, muscle, and fat—AI can identify conditions like sarcopenia, cachexia, or osteoporosis from routine imaging (Al-Sawaf et al., 2023; Elhakim et al., 2023; Pickhardt et al., 2013).

Generative AI has become increasingly prominent in medical imaging, with diffusion models, generative adversarial networks, and other approaches being used for reconstruction, registration, outlier detection, disease detection, classification, and segmentation. Automated machine learning now allows clinicians without coding experience to generate AI models from data and annotations. Modern tools like ChatGPT and AI code editors enable algorithm development through natural language commands.

Kalpathy-Cramer outlined 10 challenges facing AI implementation in clinical settings:

- *Generalizability*. AI models tend to be brittle, working well on training data but poorly on external datasets, particularly across different populations or disease presentations.
- *Shortcut Learning*. Models excel at finding patterns that lack practical clinical utility. For example, some studies claiming to predict risk of Parkinson's or Alzheimer's disease using fundus images had actually learned age as a proxy rather than true disease markers.
- *Model Repeatability*. Retesting the same patient does not always yield consistent results.
- *Calibration*. Model scores often do not correlate appropriately with actual disease risk.
- *Silent Failures*. Models may be "confidently wrong," failing without indication.
- *Explainability and Interpretability*. Black-box nature makes it difficult to understand how models reach conclusions.
- *Bias*. Models can exhibit bias in ways that are hard to detect.
- *Incorrect Metrics*. Finding appropriate evaluation metrics is challenging, particularly for low-prevalence conditions where accuracy is inadequate.
- *Incorrect Ground Truth*. Determining true "ground truth" is difficult when human experts disagree on diagnoses.
- *Inadequate Testing and Validation*. Field validation remains insufficient for safe clinical deployment.

Kalpathy-Cramer then discussed the recently developed FUTURE-AI consensus framework, which calls for AI tools that are "fair, universal, traceable, usable, robust, and explainable" throughout the development cycle (Lekadir et al., 2025). The framework provides a comprehensive checklist covering four phases: design, development, evaluation, and deployment.

Key pre-development questions include the following: Will the model work on different scanners and populations? Does it have out-of-distribution detection? Is it well calibrated? Does it make grave errors? The framework also addresses whether to use single federated models (i.e., models that are trained across decentralized databases or other data sources) or locally adapted ones, acknowledging trade-offs between general applicability and local optimization.

Kalpathy-Cramer referenced a recent Food and Drug Administration publication highlighting key challenges in AI regulation and implementation (Warraich et al., 2025). The paper emphasized preparing for unknowns in large language models and generative AI; understanding the importance of AI lifecycle management; balancing roles among big tech, startups, and academia; and addressing tensions between financial optimization and health outcomes improvement.

These considerations represent ongoing challenges that the radiology community continues to address as AI becomes increasingly integrated into clinical practice. The path forward demands careful attention to validation, safety, and ethical implementation to realize AI's potential while minimizing risks to patient care.

Replacing CT with Quantitative Magnetic Resonance Imaging

Cameron Piron, co-founder and president of Synaptive Medical, outlined how improvements in magnetic resonance imaging (MRI) technology combined with AI are enabling MRI to replace CT across many medical applications. His journey began with founding Sentinelle Medical, which focused on developing MRI technology to replace mammography for early cancer detection.

While MRI images were more expensive and complex than two-dimensional mammograms, and radiologists had to transition from reading single images to thousands of three-dimensional, multi-parametric datasets with contrast injection, the increased tumor detectability provided an advantage. Over time, his company optimized magnetic resonance (MR) images, shortened scan times, and added early AI analytics to facilitate tumor detection. Today, MRI is used for breast cancer detection at thousands of sites.

Near the end of his tenure at Sentinelle, the company began using MRI to detect responsive tumors in late-stage cancer patients. Working with the National Institutes of Health and the National Cancer Institute (NCI), they used multi-parametric MRI to detect very small tumor changes in response to different chemotherapy doses before surgery, demonstrating MRI's value across different points in the patient care cycle. The progression into Synaptive Medical builds complete MRI systems designed for neurosurgery. "We have hundreds of sites using robotics and MR data being integrated into better patient planning [and] into better navigation procedures," Piron said.

Making MRI more accessible has been key to replacing CT, he said. The machines are both smaller and less expensive than earlier versions. The INOVAIT program, a Canadian multicenter collaboration between academic centers and companies, exemplifies this accessibility by using AI to improve image-guided therapy. Piron argued that the combination of AI and MRI provides doctors with superior images for both diagnosis and surgical guidance, leading to rapidly growing demand for neurological MRI applications that now exceeds available supply.

Synaptive Medical focuses on mid-field (~0.5 T) MRI rather than traditional high-field (1.5–3.0 T) systems. While improvements traditionally came from increasing magnetic field strength, mid-field machines offer many advantages without sacrificing performance. They have demonstrated equivalent imaging performance to high-field systems while providing additional benefits.

Piron explained that the growth in MRI usage in neurology stems from various advances, including stereotactic accuracy capabilities. For brain imaging, particularly in pediatric and developmental areas, an enormous shift away from CT has occurred due to concerns about radiation exposure risks in young patients including in areas related to stroke detection, psychiatric applications, and Alzheimer's disease.

Traditionally, MRI relied on very high-field machines that were complex, heavy, and difficult to use—complexity that hindered consistent and reproducible AI analytics. By decreasing field strength and system complexity without compromising performance, Synaptive has achieved previously unseen results.

Mid-field MRI eliminates temporal variability issues present in high-field systems. While 3.0 tesla (T) machines typically show 10–14 percent variability in structure measurements over time, 0.5 T systems avoid these effects. Piron explained that this results in temporal variability nearly an order of magnitude lower than high-field machines, which is "absolutely essential for complex AI analysis when we want to be able to do more with smaller patient datasets."

Piron ended his remarks by explaining that AI enables MRI use in traditionally challenging areas—like the sinus region, where scan times optimized to 2 minutes have the potential for AI-driven reduction to 15 seconds. He stated that these advances position AI-enhanced mid-field MRI as a versatile, accessible alternative to CT across diverse medical applications while providing superior diagnostic capabilities and the potential to reduce patient risk.

DISCUSSION

Chung began the panel discussion by asking the two speakers what new AI applications in the diagnostic imaging space they were most excited about and which they thought were ready for prime time.

Piron began by saying that several applications accelerate MRI and CT. He said that anticipating unacknowledged trade-offs—things that might be missed when the time to obtain an image is significantly reduced—is important. However, he continued, one advantage of faster MRI is a reduced cost, so having an immediate return on investment is possible. What he is most excited about, he continued, is new ways to link results across disciplines, such as linking pathology results with spatial information and imaging—in short, "the ability to get ground truth built into imaging in a way that hasn't been done before."

Kalpathy-Cramer pointed to increased quantification in imaging as an exciting development. The use of AI for segmentation, for instance, helps to quantify tumor burden on the lifespan, she said; more generally, MRI and other types of imaging can be made much more quantitative than they have been. "We have the technology now," she said. "We just need to start deploying it."

Chung followed up by asking, What should vendors be doing in the quality assurance and quality control area, and what should they be revealing to end users about the acceleration techniques? Piron expressed his feeling that vendors do not seem to be doing enough in that space. The systems have become more opaque and less accessible at a time when much more visibility is important so that users can understand what is going on. "There needs to be a really definitive pushback to . . . let people see what's happening behind the algorithms so that we can have that trust," he said.

Kalpathy-Cramer agreed, saying that users need to know what data were used in training a model, what the model characteristics are, and where the model is likely to break. The data used in training the model are a particularly important factor, she continued, because if the people whose data were used to train a model are significantly different from the people that the model will be used to examine, the model's results can be wildly inaccurate. One approach to supplying the necessary data would be to use model cards (a document that provides detailed, transparent information about an AI model), she said.

Chung continued by asking about model cards: Several model card templates exist, she noted. What information should be included on a model card? Kalpathy-Cramer answered that a model card should have information not only on the demographics of the population that the model was trained on but also much more, including such things as the spectrum of disease, anatomical variations, disease presentations, and population differences. "So," she concluded, "we need biology plus all these other things."

In response to a question from Chung on the future of generative AI and large language models in general medical diagnosis, Kalpathy-Cramer said that she is very excited about it, but concerns exist for a good reason. "Until we can have sufficient guardrails and until we have the technology that allows us to figure out when there are hallucinations or when there are other things, I think we still have to be a little cautious," she said.

Another question, Kalpathy-Cramer continued, relates to how the accuracy and performance of various models should be balanced with the need for human explanation. If no explanation is provided for how a model reaches its results, monitoring the model's performance is more difficult, but some models seem to work well despite the absence of an explanation of how the model is getting its answers. For instance, some AI models predict the risk of developing breast cancer 5 years in the future, and they seem to work phenomenally well, but no human can assess if they are actually correct. Other models can predict the risk of heart attack by examining images of the retina, but no one knows what signal they are detecting. She pondered how we could gain trust in deploying these models that are not easy to check.

Piron added that because AI models do not come to answers in the same way that human minds do, they provide an "orthogonal" way of thinking. "You're seeing solutions coming up that are just not intuitive, but they are correct and they are logical," he said. "This is a valuable addition to the human intellectual toolbox, but it is still important to develop a way of understanding the machine logic because relying on purely black-box answers is a bit unnerving."

Chung then switched subjects to image reconstruction. Humans use AI to produce reconstructed images because images are meaningful to them, but, she continued, "these AI models can also potentially find a lot of patterns in data that we cannot necessarily appreciate." So, what data should AI models be trained on? Should they be trained on the raw data? Kalpathy-Cramer answered first: "We reconstruct it for the way we think. Is that the best way? Can we go from the raw data to the result that we want?" Chung asked whether vendors should provide the raw data in addition to the reconstructed images so that users can better understand what is happening. "Yes," Piron answered. In reconstructing MR images, for instance, one merges data up front and puts those data through a Fourier reconstruction. That process ends up filtering out a "wealth of information" that could potentially be valuable. As an example, he told a story from the early days of breast MRI. Ultrasound units, which had been the standard for detecting breast tumors, had been trained for years to highlight particular types of tumors that clinicians were familiar with, but at the same time that process made other types of tumors harder to see. When MRI was introduced, those types of tumors became detectable, and the cost of "optimizing" the ultrasound units became obvious.

Another audience question emerged: Given how AI is leading to faster screening and the ability to proactively image, could this lead to the sort of over diagnosing or overtreating of disease that prostate-specific antigen screening caused for cancer? And what can be done to avoid such overtreatment? Piron stated that in the future, much more early screening and full-body MR screening, among other actions, will likely occur, and this could clearly lead to more unnecessary procedures. This sort of screening could come with some way to improve specificity, he said: "If you do not have a perfectly specific imaging modality—which you do not—then you're going to lead to biopsies, lead to surgeries, [and] lead to everything else downstream." Watchful waiting, which is becoming an important paradigm for such screening as prostate cancer, could have to be part of the answer as well.

The session concluded with questions from the audience and discussions around utilizing AI in imaging and radiation therapy.

RADIATION THERAPY AND ONCOLOGY

The panel on AI in radiation therapy and oncology was co-moderated by Anyi Li, chief of computer service at Memorial Sloan Kettering Cancer Center, and Ceferino Obcemea, program director of medical physics at the Radiation Research Program at NCI. As context, Li noted that the doses that radiation oncologists use in their treatments are larger and more acute than the doses used in imaging and those generally experienced outside of a medical setting, but the exposures in radiation therapy are more tightly focused.

AI Agents for Adaptive Radiotherapy

The first speaker was Steve Jiang, vice chair of digital health and AI and chief of the Medical Physics and Engineering Division at the University of Texas Southwestern. His presentation was about using AI agents for adaptive radiotherapy (ART).

Radiotherapy is one of the three major cancer treatment options alongside surgery and chemotherapy. Jiang provided an overview statistical example that for much of the past century, patients received conventional treatment doses of about 2 gray (Gy) per day over several weeks, totaling 60–70 Gy. Stereotactic body radiotherapy, developed about a decade ago, uses higher doses of around 18 Gy delivered every 1–3 days for a total of about 54 Gy. However, both approaches are one-size-fits-all, with patients in the same cohort receiving identical treatment without interruption. Furthermore, radiologists monitor only for acute toxicity, assessing benefits and harms long after treatment completion when changes are no longer possible.

According to Jiang, several treatment variables could be adjusted to personalize treatments, including the number of fractions, radiation amount per dose, time between fractions, and total fractions. While radiologists typically keep these variables constant across cohorts, personalization involves choosing values that reflect each individual's unique needs and situation.

Jiang identified two dimensions of personalized radiotherapy. The first involves determining an individual's treatment course up front based on biomarkers, tumor characteristics, and patient health status. The second dimension adapts treatment based on ongoing tumor response and patient status, using anatomical imaging (i.e., MRI, CT) to assess changes in tumor size and shape, examining biomarkers to evaluate tissue response, and employing functional imaging to assess metabolic activity changes. However, this second dimension remains largely unexplored.

Imaging-based ART can be characterized as Generation 1 or Generation 2. Generation 1 ART aims to maximize tumor control and minimize toxicity based on anatomic changes like tumor shrinkage and organ relationships. This approach functions more as course correction than true adaptation, with incremental overall impact. Generation 2 ART modifies treatment in real time based on tumor and patient response. While still maximizing tumor control and minimizing toxicity, the prescription changes in response to the patient's body dynamics. "It is a true feedback mechanism in a control theory model," Jiang explained. "It is true adaptation, and I believe that is the future of cancer radiotherapy."

Moving from current image-guided radiotherapy to ART presents significant challenges including increased workloads, workflow complexity, technological complexity, decision-making challenges, error risks from frequent plan modifications, coordination difficulties under time pressure, and real-time decision-making requirements. ART also demands increased resources—more skilled personnel, longer treatment sessions, and continuous monitoring—which makes AI incredibly useful.

Jiang continued by explaining that various AI technologies are important for Generation 1 ART, including image acquisition, processing, segmentation, adaptation decision making, treatment planning and replanning, quality assessment, and delivery. Many commercial auto-segmentation products based on deep learning models are now available.

He said that for Generation 2 ART, AI becomes even more critical due to more severe challenges. "The decision making involves many more variables—indeed, far more than what human doctors can handle," Jiang noted. The workflow is "very resource-demanding, very complex, and tedious, so you need AI to automate the workflow," he added.

The main challenge for Generation 2 ART is insufficient appropriate data. Because past treatments have been uniform, an inadequate data spectrum exists to train AI models on outcomes for different fractions, doses, and timing variables. To address these challenges, Jiang's group is developing an AI assistant for ART based on AI agents. This assistant works alongside clinicians throughout treatment to retrieve, process, analyze, and present information for decision making while automating and streamlining clinical workflow. The assistant collaborates with multiple AI agents that can work together, use tools, make function calls for task-specific AI models, utilize clinical software tools, and access clinical databases.

Jiang distinguished between AI tools and AI agents. AI tools, like supervised deep learning models, are relatively simple input-to-output mappings—that is, "more like fitting a complex mathematical function with a deep neural network." In contrast, he said that AI agents "can perceive, think, reason, make decisions, take actions, and use tools to enhance their abilities."

His University of Texas Southwestern team is developing a multi-agent AI system featuring an AI assistant working with clinicians and a team of communicating AI agents. Key agents include a data collection and integration agent that gathers patient data from electronic health records, oncology information systems, treatment planning systems, and machine data, and then processes, curates, and indexes this information for other agents' use.

The system provides various AI agents with access to tool sets, including clinical software collections, task-specific AI models, and other tools, plus a knowledge database containing clinical guidelines, procedures, and scientific literature. Additional agents handle communication (i.e., processing spoken requests about patient history, diagnosis, or previous treatment doses), patient matching with clinical trials, real-time monitoring, automated chart preparation, clinical documentation assistance, workflow streamlining, AI-driven treatment recommendations, error detection, and patient question answering.

Jiang discussed how single AI models are insufficient for clinical deployment. Clinically viable solutions involve compound, integrated AI systems that combine AI tools, AI agents, software tools, and databases. For example, accurate auto-segmentation requires more than just an auto-segmentation model—it needs deployment and adaptation agents for acceptance testing, model commissioning, and local alignment; segmentation workflow agents; performance review agents; and monitoring agents to track model performance over time and address data drift. Similarly, decision-support AI systems involve multiple agents including predictive AI models, clinical dashboard and visualization agents, predictive modeling and case-based reasoning agents, AI expert collaboration agents, and clinical guidelines and literature agents.

Response-based ART enables fully personalized radiotherapy with longitudinal adaptation. Jiang stated that AI may be essential for workflow automation, clinical decision support, and quality assurance to ensure scalable and clinically viable ART. Single AI models cannot handle ART's complexity; instead, compound AI systems integrating agents, clinical software tools, databases, and AI models provide practical solutions for the future of cancer radiotherapy.

Multi-omics Integration for Healthcare Applications

Lei Xing, professor of radiation oncology and medical physics at Stanford University, discussed the use of AI in integrating multiple omics for use in healthcare and, specifically, precision medicine.

Xing outlined that AI for precision medicine rests on three pillars: computing resources, AI models, and data. While data can be evaluated across multiple dimensions—amount, quality, and format—his focus centers on format optimization. Healthcare data exist in diverse formats including images, pathology reports, and electronic health records and often suffer from noise, small sample sizes, and missing data.

The challenge lies in tabular data, which, despite being familiar through Excel spreadsheets, represent one of the most difficult formats for AI agents to process, particularly with large omics datasets. Xing's team developed an innovative solution: converting tabular data into images that AI can analyze more effectively (Yan et al., 2025).

Using single-cell RNA sequencing data as an example—a common biology laboratory output—Xing described the typical data structure as a massive table with columns representing individual cells and rows representing genes (can be on the order of 10,000 genes per cell). Each cell contains read counts for specific gene–cell combinations.

The key breakthrough involves converting gene expression vectors into optimized image representations called genomaps. A vector can be converted into an image in many ways, Xing noted. His group's technique accounts for gene–gene interactions to optimally place genes into pixels, ensuring each cell converts into a meaningful image rather than random noise.

He noted that different cell types produce distinct patterns in their genomap representations—patterns so clear that visual inspection alone can distinguish cell types without AI assistance. However, when analyzed through convolutional neural networks (CNNs), these image representations significantly outperform traditional one-dimensional vector approaches.

The genomaps serve as the foundation for a comprehensive analytical pipeline. Individual cell data convert into genomaps, which then feed into GenoNet, a CNN performing deep-level feature extraction. This system enables multiple downstream applications including cell recognition, cell-specific gene set discovery, trajectory mapping, multi-omics integration, dimensionality reduction, visualization, and clustering.

Xing's team successfully applied this approach to radiation oncology and radiology, specifically with radiomics data. Converting tabular radiomics data into images and analyzing them with CNNs improved survival prediction and biomarker discovery accuracy by 10–20 percent over existing methods. The technique reveals temporal patterns, showing how cells at different ages display distinct representations and how lung fibrosis cells change appearance before and after radiation treatment.

Spatial transcriptomics represents another application area, where the method combines morphology and molecular information for cancer subtyping and gene mutation prediction. The genomaps concept extends beyond individual applications, serving as a method for incorporating physical understanding into data representations. This enhanced data understanding proves valuable for training models and fine-tuning large foundation models.

A recent application demonstrates this integration through GPT-4Vision (Liu et al., 2024), an automated treatment planning framework developed by Xing's team. This system incorporates both tabular data and dose-volume histograms to evaluate radiotherapy treatment plans and provide textual feedback for plan improvements. Looking forward, Xing's team is developing a multimodal and multiscale foundation model that incorporates relationships among data and modalities, creating more powerful and useful systems than current foundation models.

By converting tabular biomedical data into optimized image representations, Xing's genomaps approach addresses a fundamental challenge in medical AI. The technique's consistent 10–20 percent accuracy improvements across diverse applications—from single-cell analysis to radiation oncology—demonstrate its broad utility. As the field moves toward integrated foundation models and multi-agent systems, this data format optimization serves as a crucial building block for more effective precision medicine applications.

Xing ended by stating that this work exemplifies how addressing seemingly technical challenges in data representation can yield substantial improvements in clinical AI applications, bridging the gap between complex biological data and actionable medical insights.

DISCUSSION

Obcemea began the discussion by asking Xing about the spatially semantic topographic maps he constructs. "Most of us are familiar with the clustering technique of K nearest neighbors," Obcemea said, "but this is so much more because it is on the semantic scale." He continued that he tends to think of the approach in terms of the tabular data being a multidimensional Rubik's cube that one manipulates in order to extract a pattern. In supervised learning, he said, one extracts a pattern by doing a steep descent, which is a criterion. However, he asked, with unsupervised learning, what sort of criteria does one apply in order to get to that pattern discovery?

Xing replied that he liked that analogy. He explained that his approach amounts to reshuffling the data: "It is actually surprising to us just by simply reshuffling the data in a meaningful format, in a meaningful way, that you can get so much more information out of the data." In his team's approach, the interaction among the data elements is encoded into the spatial configuration of the data. "So, in a way, it is like clustering," he explained. "If you can cluster them first, you can throw away a lot of data in the reclustering."

The image is the key to his approach. "I'm a physicist," he said. "I see everything as an image." So he incorporates the interaction pattern into the image and then analyzes it with a CNN. "CNN is a very powerful tool," he said, "but your pattern has to have some semantic meaning. So that's what we did—we assigned some semantic meaning to the data." This same approach should be workable for other types of data, even images, he said. Some people might not think that one could get much additional information by turning an image into another image, he said, "but we are doing it. We are trying to get more semantic information for imaging data, but I do not want to go into too much technical detail."

Following up, Obcemea asked Xing for further details on how spatially semantic topographic maps extract a useful figure from a blur and how one can be certain that the extracted figure corresponds to something real—to a "ground truth." One solution, Xing said, is to add a condition. In the work that his team does, for instance, biological knowledge can be used as a condition. Thus, in the case of clustering, which is unsupervised learning, one must apply biological or clinical knowledge to understand what the model has produced. "Sometimes it may not make sense," he said, "and then you have to think, What's going on in the pipeline? So that's why I keep saying that human knowledge is the key. It is not only in the construction of this topographic representation but also in the whole pipeline." AI will always come up with an answer, he said, and then people digest and understand the answer and make it trustworthy.

Li asked Jiang about the use of agents. In healthcare, he said, the accuracy of an agent is crucial, and a single mistake can be life-threatening. Then if one uses multiple agents, errors could propagate or even be made exponentially worse. He asked, "What sorts of guardrails can be put in place to minimize the effects of such errors?" Jiang answered, "This is a very important question," particularly in cases where a multi-agent AI system in in place. One way his team minimizes errors in its agents is by building the entire system from the bottom up, step by step, and doing a very thorough validation of each individual AI model to make sure that it works. Furthermore, individual agents are not used immediately in a multi-agent system but are first thoroughly vetted. For instance, the patient–trial matching agent that his team developed is being deployed clinically, but he said that "right now, it is more like an assistant to human clinical research coordinators." It will take a while of using this agent and checking its recommendations to have enough confidence in it to embed it in a multi-agent system, he said. Furthermore, since accuracy is important when AI is used clinically, researchers and users could quantify the certainty in a system's answers so that the AI system knows what it knows and does not know.

Finally, Jiang continued, AI systems need redundancy. One can check the accuracy of a large individual model by, for instance, having multiple models working on the same task. And in the case of a chatbot that answers questions, he said, one should not rely just on a pretrained model to give accurate answers to clinical questions; rather, the answers should be grounded in clinical guidelines and the literature.

Xing added that having an agent that serves as a quality officer is important. "You're building a human society using computer agents," he said, "so a lot of key components in the clinic need to be clearly reflected in the agent world." Quality assurance is one of those components that is important in a multi-agent system.

The session ended with multiple questions from the audience focusing on specific applications for each speaker.

RADIATION OCCUPATIONAL HEALTH

The panel on AI in radiation occupational health was chaired by Sylvain Costes, former National Aeronautics and Space Administration (NASA) data officer for space, biological, and physical sciences.

Computational Approaches to Integrating Radiation Exposure Across the Life Course: Risks, Insights, and Innovations

Heidi Hanson, senior scientist and group lead of biostatistics and biomedical informatics at Oak Ridge National Laboratory, spoke about computational approaches for assessing radiation exposure across the life course. She described her ideal situation of having all of the data that she wanted to follow an individual across the life course, from in utero until time of death.

Hanson's fundamental premise challenges conventional exposure assessment approaches. Rather than examining single-point exposures or limited time frames, she suggested comprehensive lifetime exposure tracking. "Exposures at any time in an individual's life can play a role in what that person is experiencing currently," she explained. Early life exposures can moderate effects of later exposures, making complete exposure histories essential for understanding health outcomes.

To realize this vision, Hanson collaborated with pediatrician Shari Barkin to develop a five-step blueprint for charting life course exposures (Hanson et al., 2020):

1. Integration of datasets across the lifespan using transdisciplinary principles from engineering, statistics, communication, mathematics, and epidemiology;
2. Data science cores focusing on curation, cleaning, analysis, and modeling;
3. New approaches for modeling high-dimensional data;
4. Expansion of epidemiological methods to include systems and network modeling; and
5. Improvements in reproducibility with standardized operational measures.

Hanson's work primarily addresses the first two components, focusing on data harmonization rather than the more commonly pursued outcomes-driven AI applications in healthcare.

Electronic health data present formidable obstacles: heterogeneity across institutions, varied collection methods, and siloed storage systems. "It is very difficult to get to charting someone's trajectory across their entire life course because it is hard to link those datasets together," Hanson noted. This fragmentation highlights the importance of computational tools capable of managing large amounts of heterogeneous sensitive information while enabling longitudinal exposure assessments and geographical risk identification.

The solution involves standardized processes ensuring data harmonization produces clean, noise-free datasets suitable for trustworthy predictive algorithms. Hanson envisions this as a 10-year horizon goal requiring comprehensive computational infrastructure.

Hanson leads the MOSSAIC project (Making Outcomes Using Surveillance Data and Scalable Artificial Intelligence for Cancer), a Department of Energy–NCI partnership running for 9 years. Over the past 2 years, MOSSAIC has deployed AI tools across all U.S. Surveillance, Epidemiology, and End Results (SEER) registries, dramatically improving cancer reporting efficiency.

She explained that the project's tools automatically process pathology reports into tabular form using common data models. Currently, these tools autocode 23–27 percent of all pathology reports entering SEER registries. When confidence levels are insufficient, reports undergo manual review. This automation contributed to reducing cancer reporting time from 22 months to 14 months across all SEER registries.

Hanson stated that these tools demonstrate flexibility across data types and institutions. The Department of Veterans Affairs (VA) successfully adapted MOSSAIC's hierarchical self-attention model for VA electronic health records, proving cross-institutional applicability essential for standardized health record information extraction.

Scaling to national levels involves federated learning approaches, but privacy protection presents significant obstacles. While federated learning inherently protects individual data, it does not provide sufficient privacy guarantees for personal health information. "There has to be some sort of privacy mechanism imposed as you're doing the federated learning," Hanson explained.

However, privacy enhancements create accuracy trade-offs. When implementing differential privacy for NCI cancer prediction models, she said that accuracy dropped to unacceptable levels: "By turning on differential privacy, at least for the tests that we've seen, we get a considerable drop in accuracy." Hanson's team collaborates with mathematicians to address this challenge, but considerable research remains before real-world implementation becomes viable.

She next described the Centralized Health and Exposomic Resource (C-HER), which addresses geospatial data harmonization challenges. This system provides standardized processes for data ingestion, data processing, metadata storage, ontology integration, and spatial indexing across exposure types. The goal involves developing models predicting indoor radon exposure, PM2.5 (Fine Particulate Matter, airborne particles with diameters smaller than 2.5 micrometers [μm]) exposure, and exposure–cancer relationships.

C-HER emerged from early project experiences where multiple teams processed identical data differently, producing non-reproducible results. The centralized approach provides spatially indexed data in "stackable hexes," enabling rapid model development for various exposure predictions.

Through MOSSAIC, Hanson's team accessed LexisNexis residential history data for 11 SEER registries, enabling 25-year retrospective environmental exposure linking to cancer patients. This capability allows assessment of how indoor radon exposure across life periods affects treatment outcomes.

Hanson's most ambitious project, EHRLICH (Electronic Health Record–Informed Lagrangian method for precision publiC Health), aims to create computational capabilities for rapid real-world data assimilation supporting digital twins of population-level biological threats. EHRLICH employs scalable, trustworthy AI with synthetic data generation for enhanced privacy protection, using datasets completely devoid of personal health information.

Beyond residential history analysis, EHRLICH includes tools simulating individual daily movement patterns, enabling uncertainty assessment across exposure types rather than simple residential location assignments. This approach provides more nuanced exposure modeling reflecting actual human behavior patterns.

Hanson's "big dream" involves placing "a pulse on population health" through interoperable computational tools, enabling comprehensive human health understanding. Her work demonstrates that achieving precision medicine involves foundational advances in data harmonization and integration, not just sophisticated predictive algorithms.

Patient-Centric Synthetic Data Generation

The next speaker, Pierre-Antoine Gourraud, university professor and hospital practitioner at the Faculty of Medicine at the University of Nantes, expanded on a topic that Hanson introduced in the previous presentation: generating synthetic data to preserve patient privacy while still allowing for the types of analyses that are crucial in making advances in healthcare.

Gourraud started by discussing his 2023 publication in *npj Digital Medicine*, which he believes fundamentally challenges current approaches to biomedical data analysis by arguing that patient-centric synthetic data generation eliminates the need for risky personal health data usage, even in anonymized form (Guillaudeux et al., 2023). "There is no reason to risk re-identification in biomedical data analysis because synthetic data offers an effective replacement," he asserted. He described this as opening "a new era where we actually are going to all use anonymous, synthetic, and probably augmented datasets."

He then discussed the development of synthetic health data and how it has been accelerated by Europe's stringent privacy regulations. The General Data Protection Regulation (GDPR), a comprehensive data protection law in the European Union, defines three health data categories: personal data, pseudonymous data with direct identifiers removed, and truly anonymous data proven impossible to link to individuals. Under GDPR, data controllers must prove anonymity by answering three critical questions: Can individuals be singled out? Can records be linked to individuals? Can information be inferred about individuals?

Gourraud manages a biomedical data warehouse containing more than 100 million text documents from 3 million patients. When exporting data beyond the warehouse, he must prove complete anonymity. His synthetic data generation method enables negative answers to all three GDPR questions, ensuring true anonymization.

Gourraud's team developed Avatar, a method transforming original data into functionally equivalent but completely anonymous synthetic data. Avatar-generated data possess three essential properties: structural identity (same granularity, statistical units, observations, variables, and types as original data), analytical relevance (producing comparable results to original data), and indistinguishability (neither experts nor algorithms can differentiate synthetic from original data).

The Avatar process creates individual models for each observation in the original dataset. For each row in a data table, the method defines mathematically a set of neighbor rows—typically 12—that closely resemble the original. These neighbors form a local model containing no original data, only similar data points. Within this local model, he said, a single simulation occurs: "It is a little bit counterintuitive because you do a private local model that is used only once, and the very link you're trying to destroy, you're going to use it just to measure how many other simulations are actually closer from the original observation than the one you just sampled."

Gourraud's first major application involved a study on intracranial aneurysm rupture risk factors. When colleagues requested open science publication including data sharing, privacy concerns initially prevented pseudonymous data release. He noted that the Avatar method generated simulations for approximately 2,300 observations, creating "the exact same spreadsheet, the exact same table, same number of variables, same type of variables, [and] same types of rows, by selecting the hyperparameters that were very important to see what balance we can get between accuracy and privacy." He stated that the resulting synthetic dataset maintained analytical integrity while eliminating personal health information risks, enabling full open science publication.

Another application involved developing a clinical decision-support system for multiple sclerosis treatment. The AI tool selects reference patients from databases combining clinical trial and observational study data, identifying patients with similar characteristics to support treatment decisions. Neurologists reported identical results whether using synthetic or real data for clinical decisions. Detailed validation by Gourraud's PhD student confirmed that synthetic data performed equivalently to real data across all tool applications and population subgroups. The synthetic approach delivered identical clinical outcomes without privacy compromise.

Beyond privacy-protected analysis, synthetic health data enable multiple applications. Data sharing becomes feasible through "sandboxes" where potential partners can explore synthetic datasets to demonstrate intended usage without accessing real patient information. Educational applications benefit significantly, providing students with challenging, realistic datasets for learning without privacy concerns. Software testing traditionally requires real data but becomes safer using synthetic alternatives.

Gourraud frames synthetic data generation as fundamentally ethical: "There is no reason to risk re-identification if the patient is not using or the caregiver is actually not directly benefiting from the analysis that we are conducting." This perspective positions privacy protection as a moral imperative rather than merely regulatory compliance.

The GDPR-driven innovation model suggests broader potential for regulation-fostered advancement. Gourraud expressed conviction that "new regulation can foster worldwide innovation that indeed replicates individual data," extending beyond European borders to global biomedical research.

Gourraud's Avatar method represents a paradigm shift from privacy-risk management to privacy-risk elimination in biomedical data analysis. By generating structurally identical, analytically relevant, and truly anonymous synthetic data, the approach enables full scientific openness without compromising patient privacy.

The success in clinical applications—from aneurysm research to multiple sclerosis treatment support—demonstrates practical viability. As regulatory frameworks worldwide increasingly emphasize data protection, Gourraud's synthetic data generation offers a pathway forward that simultaneously advances scientific progress and upholds ethical standards.

He ended his remarks highlighting how this innovation exemplifies how regulatory constraints can catalyze technological advancement, transforming compliance challenges into opportunities for methodological breakthroughs that benefit both research communities and patient populations.

DISCUSSION

Costes opened the discussion session by asking how the presenters' tools address the issue of data silos and transform diverse data sources into formats ready for AI.

Hanson began by describing her team's work with unstructured text data from national cancer registries across six to seven states. She explained that data are collected differently at every site, requiring extensive data engineering tools to create harmonized structures. "We try to develop a set of rules that can be applied across all the different datasets," she said, noting that they hope model training will address remaining heterogeneity. Her team is now transitioning to structured data from electronic health records, which she described as more difficult than unstructured data work.

When Costes asked about scalability from state-level to national questions and similarly asked Gourraud about scaling from university hospitals to entire countries, the responses revealed significant challenges. Gourraud explained that coordination exists among university hospitals nationally, with the key issue being data exchange. "That's how we got interested in anonymous synthetic data, because the best way is actually to show the data," he said, noting that data exchange can begin discussions about converging on comparable formats.

Hanson was frank about scaling limitations: "No, we're not ready to scale up. As optimistic as I am, what I've also noticed as we've brought on new datasets is even if they are very similar in nature, there are 'gotchas' as you start to process the data [including] characters that you didn't expect to be in there." She believes scaling is possible but acknowledged that "it will take work to get there."

The discussion shifted to synthetic data when Costes relayed audience questions about preserving correlations between features in multimodal datasets. Gourraud answered affirmatively, but Hanson disagreed, stating that the complexity of multimodal modeling would necessitate the creation of comprehensive synthetic datasets equivalent to human population datasets, which is not yet attainable. Gourraud countered by highlighting his Avatar program's robustness with heterogeneous populations containing multiple subpopulations. "Most of the time when my colleagues come with a dataset, they have actually three, four, [or] five different subpopulations," he said, explaining that the method automatically uses local models for subgroups, which makes it "extremely robust and extremely useful for hypothesis generation."

Regarding a question on democratizing healthcare data access, Hanson suggested combining federated learning with synthetic data. "It is the combination of both of those that I think is really innovative and really going to lead us to cool places in the future," she said. Gourraud agreed, noting that even with perfect synthetic data, controlling institutional data use makes federated learning important.

Costes then asked about privacy concerns in federated learning. Hanson identified membership inference attacks as basic concerns, explaining that "there are a couple of repositories online where you can reconstruct data from the gradients that you're passing back and forth in a federated learning run, and it is a shockingly small amount of code that gets you to that recreation."

The discussion moved to handling outliers in synthetic data. Gourraud explained that this is very difficult because "somebody who stands out of the crowd is somebody that you are going to re-identify." The solution involves bringing outliers "back into the pack," and when outliers form subgroups, generating more synthetic outliers than existed originally. His group generates "at least 10 times as much synthetic data as the original data."

Hanson noted problems with synthetic data approaches depending on purpose. For predictive models, overinflating minority classes might improve performance while protecting privacy, but for population assessments requiring unchanged distributions, "overinflating those minority classes may lead to a problem in what I'm trying to estimate," she explained.

When Costes asked about inappropriate synthetic data uses, Hanson stated she does not believe synthetic data are ready for hypothesis generation because correlation structures must be protected. Gourraud countered that in many situations, "it is either synthetic data or nothing," and he suggested using synthetic data with subsequent validation against original datasets.

On integrating mechanistic models with AI, Gourraud emphasized focusing on data rather than algorithms: "Rather than being in the hype of 'let's try the newest model or AI algorithm,' I think we're both big believers in data, [so] that's where we're putting our efforts." Hanson expressed preference for multiple approaches over one-size-fits-all solutions suggesting triangulation with different models. "I think that you can use mechanistic models to help you identify where there should be guardrails on some of what we're doing with AI," she said, emphasizing the goal of combining models.

Finally, Costes asked about establishing consortiums for data standardization. Hanson supported this but cautioned against rule development–focused groups, instead favoring those that "start to think about how we can identify technological solutions that will allow us to standardize and harmonize the data." Gourraud agreed: "I think it is great to have the ambition of having standards, but we have to remember that they are a means to an end, and that it is by doing projects [and] by being grounded into practical examples that are useful for patients and for caregivers that we will succeed."

REFERENCES

Al-Sawaf, O., J. Weiss, M. Skrzypski, J. M. Lam, T. Karasaki, F. Zambrana, A. C. Kidd, A. M. Frankell, T. B. K. Watkins, C. Martínez-Ruiz, C. Puttick, J. R. M. Black, A. Huebner, M. A. Bakir, M. Sokač, S. Collins, S. Veeriah, N. Magno, C. Naceur-Lombardelli, P. Prymas, A. Toncheva, S. Ward, N. Jayanth, R. Salgado, C. P. Bridge, D. C. Christiani, R. H. Mak, C. Bay, M. Rosenthal, N. Sattar, P. Welsh, Y. Liu, N. Perrimon,

K. Popuri, M. F. Beg, N. McGranahan, A. Hackshaw, D.M. Breen, S. O'Rahilly, N. J. Birkbak, H. J. W. L. Aerts, the TRACERx Consortium, M. Jamal-Hanjani, and C. Swanton. 2023. Body composition and lung cancer-associated cachexia in TRACERx. *Nature Medicine* 29(4):846–858.

Beers, A., J. Brown, K. Chang, K. Hoebel, J. Patel, K. I. Ly, S. M. Tolaney, P. Brastianos, B. Rosen, E. R. Gerstner, and J. Kalpathy-Cramer. 2021. DeepNeuro: An open-source deep learning toolbox for neuroimaging. *Neuroinformatics* 19(1):127–140.

Chang, K., A. L. Beers, H. X. Bai, J. M. Brown, K. I. Ly, X. Li, J. T. Senders, V. K. Kavouridis, A. Boaro, C. Su, W. L. Bi, O. Rapalino, W. Liao, Q. Shen, H. Zhou, B. Xiao, Y. Wang, P. J. Zhang, M. C. Pinho, P. Y. Wen, T. T. Batchelor, J. L. Boxerman, O. Arnaout, B. R. Rosen, E. R. Gerstner, L. Yang, R. Y. Huang, and J. Kalpathy-Cramer. 2019. Automatic assessment of glioma burden: A deep learning algorithm for fully automated volumetric and bidimensional measurement. *Neuro-Oncology* 21(11):1412–1422.

Elhakim, T., K. Trinh, A. Mansur, C. Bridge, and D. Daye. 2023. Role of machine learning–based CT body composition in risk prediction and prognostication: Current state and future directions. *Diagnostics (Basel)* 13(5):968.

Elhalawani, H., B. Elgohari, T. A. Lin, A. S. R. Mohamed, T. J. Fitzgerald, F. Laurie, K. Ulin, J. Kalpathy-Cramer, T. Guerrero, E. B. Holliday, G. Russo, A. Patel, W. Jones, G. V. Walker, M. Awan, M. Choi, R. Dagan, O. Mahmoud, A. Shapiro, F. S. Kong, D. Gomez, J. Zeng, R. Decker, F. O. B. Spoelstra, L. E. Gaspar, L. A. Kachnic, C. R. Thomas Jr., P. Okunieff, and C. D. Fuller. 2019. An in-silico quality assurance study of contouring target volumes in thoracic tumors within a cooperative group setting. *Clinical and Translational Radiation Oncology* 15:83–92.

Guillaudeux, M., O. Rousseau, J. Petot, Z. Bennis, C. A. Dein, T. Goronflot, N. Vince, S. Limou, M. Karakachoff, M. Wargny, and P. A. Gourraud. 2023. Patient-centric synthetic data generation, no reason to risk re-identification in biomedical data analysis. *npj Digital Medicine* 6(1):37.

Hanson, H. A., C. L. Leiser, G. Bandoli, B. H. Pollock, M. R. Karagas, D. Armstrong, A. Dozier, N. G. Weiskopf, M. Monaghan, A. M. Davis, E. Eckstrom, C. Weng, J. N. Tobin, F. Kaskel, M. R. Schleiss, P. Szilagyi, C. Dykes, D. Cooper, and S. L. Barkin. 2020. Charting the life course: Emerging opportunities to advance scientific approaches using life course research. *Journal of Clinical and Translational Science* 5(1):e9.

Koetzier, L. R., D. Mastrodicasa, T. P. Szczykutowicz, N. R. van der Werf, A. S. Wang, V. Sandfort, A. J. van der Molen, D. Fleischmann, and M. J. Willemink. 2023. Deep learning image reconstruction for CT: Technical principles and clinical prospects. *Radiology* 306(3):e221257.

Lekadir, K., A. F. Frangi, A. R. Porras, B. Glocker, C. Cintas, C. P. Langlotz, E. Weicken, F. W. Asselbergs, F. Prior, G. S. Collins, G. Kaissis, G. Tsakou, I. Buvat, J. Kalpathy-Cramer, J. Mongan, J. A. Schnabel, K. Kushibar, K. Riklund, K. Marias, L. M. Amugongo, L. A. Fromont, L. Maier-Hein, L. Cerdá-Alberich, L. Martí-Bonmatí, M. J. Cardoso, M. Bobowicz, M. Shabani, M. Tsiknakis, M. A. Zuluaga, M. C. Fritzsche, M. Camacho, M. G. Linguraru, M. Wenzel, M. De Bruijne, M. G. Tolsgaard, M. Goisauf, M. Cano Abadía, N. Papanikolaou, N. Lazrak, O. Pujol, R. Osuala, S. Napel, S. Colantonio, S. Joshi, S. Klein, S. Aussó, W. A. Rogers, Z. Salahuddin, M. P. A. Starmans, and the FUTURE-AI Consortium. 2025. FUTURE-AI: International consensus guideline for trustworthy and deployable artificial intelligence in healthcare. *BMJ* 388:e081554.

Liu, S., O. Pastor-Serrano, Y. Chen, M. Gopaulchan, W. Liang, M. Buyyounouski, E. Pollom, Q. T. Le, M. Gensheimer, P. Dong, Y. Yang, J. Zou, and L. Xing. 2024. Automated radiotherapy treatment planning guided by GPT-4Vision. *ArXiv* [Preprint]. Jul 1:arXiv:2406.15609v2.

Ng, S. P., B. A. Dyer, J. Kalpathy-Cramer, A. S. R. Mohamed, M. J. Awan, G. B. Gunn, J. Phan, M. Zafereo, J. M. Debnam, C. M. Lewis, R. R. Colen, M. E. Kupferman, N. Guha-Thakurta, G. Canahuate, G. E. Marai,

D. Vock, B. Hamilton, J. Holland, C. E. Cardenas, S. Lai, D. Rosenthal, and C. D. Fuller. 2018. A prospective in silico analysis of interdisciplinary and interobserver spatial variability in post-operative target delineation of high-risk oral cavity cancers: Does physician specialty matter? *Clinical and Translational Radiation Oncology* 12:40–46.

Peng, J., D. D. Kim, J. B. Patel, X. Zeng, J. Huang, K. Chang, X. Xun, C. Zhang, J. Sollee, J. Wu, D. J. Dalal, X. Feng, H. Zhou, C. Zhu, B. Zou, K. Jin, P. Y. Wen, J. L. Boxerman, K. E. Warren, T. Y. Poussaint, L. J. States, J Kalpathy-Cramer, L. Yang, R. Y. Huang, and H. X. Bai. 2022. Deep learning-based automatic tumor burden assessment of pediatric high-grade gliomas, medulloblastomas, and other leptomeningeal seeding tumors. *Neuro-Oncology* 24(2):289–299.

Pickhardt, P. J., B. D. Pooler, T. Lauder, A. M. del Rio, R. J. Bruce, and N. Binkley. 2013. Opportunistic screening for osteoporosis using abdominal computed tomography scans obtained for other indications. *Annals of Internal Medicine* 158(8):588–595.

Robinson-Weiss, C., J. Patel, B. C. Bizzo, D. I. Glazer, C. P. Bridge, K. P. Andriole, B. Dabiri, J. K. Chin, K. Dreyer, J. Kalpathy-Cramer, and W. W. Mayo-Smith. 2023. Machine learning for adrenal gland segmentation and classification of normal and adrenal masses at CT. *Radiology* 306(2):e220101.

Warraich, H. J., T. Tazbaz, and R. M. Califf. 2025. FDA perspective on the regulation of artificial intelligence in health care and biomedicine. *JAMA* 333(3):241–247.

Yan, R., M. T. Islam, and L. Xing. 2025. Interpretable discovery of patterns in tabular data via spatially semantic topographic maps. *Nature Biomedical Engineering* 9(4):471–482. https://doi.org/10.1038/s41551-024-01268-6.

4
Data for Artificial Intelligence Readiness

A session devoted to discussing the importance of data collection, curation, and management for use in artificial intelligence (AI) using examples from medical imaging as a focus to discuss this topic. This session aimed to address the aspect of the statement of task on intentionality of data collection, detector development, and dataset management for future AI and machine learning (ML) end algorithm applications. The session was moderated by Anyi Li, chief of computer service at Memorial Sloan Kettering Cancer Center, and Leo Chiang, senior research and development fellow at the Dow Chemical Company.

DATA FOR AI: THE CRITICAL ROLE OF METADATA AND CONTEXT

Caroline Chung, vice president and chief data and analytics officer, co-director of the Institute for Data Science and Oncology, and professor of radiation oncology and diagnostic imaging at the University of Texas MD Anderson Cancer Center, began the session by talking about the critical role that metadata and context play in data used for AI. Many people think about data readiness in terms of perfectly cleaned data, she said, but that sort of data may not be required "as long as you consider the context of how you're wanting to use the data."

The development of AI tools in healthcare faces a fundamental challenge that extends far beyond algorithmic sophistication. As Chung emphasized in her presentation, a significant "AI chasm" exists—that is, the gulf between developing scientifically sound algorithms and their meaningful real-world applications, as described by Keane and Topol (2018). Context, she argued, provides the critical bridge to span this chasm, transforming data science tools from laboratory curiosities into practical healthcare solutions.

She offered that the path to successful AI implementation begins with a fundamental shift in approach. Rather than asking what can be built with available data, Chung suggested starting with clearly defined problems that need to be solved. This problem-first methodology prevents the creation of sophisticated but ultimately useless "widgets" that may perform well in controlled settings but lack practical utility in clinical environments. The availability of training data does not guarantee the availability of similar data in real-world deployment, making context-aware planning essential from conception through implementation, she said. Three considerations can help guide this process: first, ensuring that model training and validation align with actual clinical needs; second, assessing stakeholder and operational readiness for implementation; and third, guaranteeing that model outputs can be communicated effectively to end users in ways they understand and trust.

Healthcare AI increasingly relies on integrating diverse data types—imaging, omics, metabolites, physiological measurements, and environmental factors. However, this integration presents significant contextual challenges that can undermine model validity. Temporal context is likely crucial: The timing of a biopsy versus omics data collection can render associations meaningless if the timescales are too separated. Similarly, spatial context matters enormously—without knowing the exact location within a tumor where a specimen was obtained, researchers risk making unfounded assumptions about the relationship between imaging findings and molecular profiles.

As Chung noted in her 2021 *Cancer Research* publication (Chung and Jaffray, 2021), metadata serve as the essential "glue" that brings observations together meaningfully. Without proper context and metadata, even rich datasets can become significantly less valuable and can lead to erroneous conclusions.

The practical implications of inadequate contextual awareness extend beyond theoretical concerns into direct patient care impacts. Chung's examination of brain magnetic resonance imaging (MRI) data from the National Cancer Institute's (NCI's) National Clinical Trials Network revealed imaging slice thicknesses ranging from 1mm to 5mm, with most using 4mm slices (Thrower et al., 2021). This variation has profound consequences: tumors visible at 1mm resolution can "disappear" when reconstructed with 3mm slices. A patient transferring between centers using different imaging protocols might suddenly appear to have stage 4 disease, potentially leading to inappropriate clinical trial enrollment based on imaging artifacts rather than disease progression.

The COVID–19 pandemic provided another stark illustration of contextual blindness. Early AI models trained to detect COVID–19 from medical images inadvertently learned to distinguish between pediatric and adult lungs rather than positive and negative cases, because most COVID–19-negative patients were children while COVID-19-positive cases were predominantly adults (Heaven, 2021). The failure to account for age metadata rendered these models fundamentally flawed.

She discussed how electronic health records (EHRs) present additional contextual challenges. Research by Steinkamp and colleagues (2022) revealed extensive copying and pasting in EHRs, propagating duplicate information and errors throughout patient records. While clinicians recognize and work around these inconsistencies through conversations and clinical judgment, data scientists accessing only the recorded information miss those conversations that inform actual medical decisions. This gap between documented and actual clinical reasoning creates significant challenges for AI model development.

Chung explained that effective healthcare AI likely involves dynamic data quality assessment based on intended use. She stated that perfect data are not always necessary—the required quality depends on the specific application. Exploratory research seeking general patterns can tolerate some noise, she elaborated, while clinical prediction models for individual patients necessitate high-quality inputs to minimize uncertainty in life-affecting decisions.

She discussed how data provenance may then be equally critical for building trust and reliability. Users need to understand data origins, cleaning processes, and any transformations applied. Chung described a cautionary example where a published dataset contained significant amounts of imputed data, but hundreds of researchers unknowingly used these artificial data because their provenance was not documented.

Chung stated that less obvious sources of bias may also be considered. Scanning frequency differences can create detection bias—patients scanned every 2 months will show progression earlier than those scanned every 6 months, potentially skewing model predictions. Measurement error bias from scanner variations, protocol differences, and patient cooperation adds additional layers of complexity that context-aware models aim to address.

Chung argued that rather than simplifying or ignoring healthcare's inherent complexity, it can be embraced as a source of deeper understanding. This approach involves considering both content (the data themselves) and context (the metadata) to enable meaningful data curation and generate genuine insights. Success likely includes starting with clearly defined purposes, building appropriate teams, assembling contextually rich datasets, and maintaining awareness of context throughout development and implementation.

The path forward likely involves robust verification, validation, and uncertainty quantification that considers both data and model limitations. Through this comprehensive approach, healthcare AI systems can build the trust and confidence to inform critical medical decisions. As healthcare continues to generate increasingly complex and diverse datasets, the ability to maintain and leverage contextual understanding will determine which AI tools successfully bridge the chasm between laboratory promise and clinical reality.

She ended with an example of how the integration of emerging technologies like ambient listening may help fill some contextual gaps, but the fundamental challenge remains: creating AI systems that understand not just what the data say but what they mean within the full complexity of healthcare delivery. This contextual awareness, supported by appropriate data governance systems ensuring proper access and attribution, forms the foundation upon which truly useful healthcare AI can be built.

REQUISITES AND CHALLENGES IN QUANTITATIVE IMAGING

Dan Sullivan, professor emeritus at the Duke University Medical Center, spoke about how to interpret quantitative imaging properly. In particular, he explained, while most of the symposium's speakers had talked about the data in large collections of scans, he focused on the issue of the data within a single image.

Sullivan started by stating that radiology has grappled with a fundamental problem for nearly a century: the persistent variability in radiologists' subjective interpretations of images across all imaging modalities and clinical applications. As Sullivan emphasized, while little can be done to improve subjective interpretations themselves, the advent of digital imaging has created unprecedented opportunities to extract objective, consistent information from medical images. This shift from subjective interpretation to quantitative measurement represents a critical evolution in medical imaging that could transform diagnostic accuracy and clinical decision making.

The magnitude of interpretive inconsistency in radiology is both striking and clinically consequential, he said. Sullivan highlighted a study by Herzog and colleagues (2017) that exemplifies this challenge. An orthopedic surgeon had a 63-year-old back pain patient receive spine MRI studies every other day for 3 weeks at 10 different New York City hospitals, revealing that no interpretive finding was reported unanimously by all radiologists and one-third of findings appeared only once. This variability indicated significant false negatives and false positives, contradicting expectations that patients should receive consistent radiologic diagnoses regardless of when and where they seek care.

Sullivan argued that if these radiologists had access to AI algorithms providing objective, quantitative information extracted from the images, the reports would likely have shown far less variation in observations and conclusions. While such AI technology is technically feasible today, its adoption remains limited, primarily due to the lack of sufficiently large training datasets for robust AI implementation in radiology.

He noted that a fundamental shift in perspective is required to fully leverage quantitative imaging potential. Sullivan emphasized that clinical images are not merely pictures but represent n-dimensional datasets where each pixel conveys information about physical or biological properties of matter. Unlike radiomics features, which are computer constructs without direct physical reality, quantitative imaging measurements correspond to actual biological and physical characteristics of tissues.

He stated that this distinction is important for understanding image interpretation as a data extraction process. When radiologists interpret images, they perform segmentation—that is, extracting subsets of overall image data, analogous to isolating and measuring specific portions of tissue. However, biological imaging inherently deals with blurry, noisy datasets. Even high-resolution scans with 1-cubic-millimeter voxels average signals from approximately 1 billion cells, creating inherent challenges in precise measurement.

Sullivan described that the clinical consequences of these measurement challenges become apparent in routine diagnostic tasks. For instance, detecting and measuring lung nodules on computed tomography (CT) scans requires identifying which pixels define the nodule's boundaries, particularly its edges. This determination directly affects size measurements, which carry significant clinical implications for patient management decisions.

Sullivan then presented on the Quantitative Imaging Biomarkers Alliance (QIBA), established by the Radiological Society of North America, which works to improve the value and practicality of quantitative imaging biomarkers (QIBs) by reducing measurement variability. QIBs provide objective quantities characterizing biological features, functioning as "imaging assays" analogous to laboratory blood tests.

Like laboratory assays, imaging assays require characterization of both technical performance—evaluated against reference objects of known characteristics—and clinical performance, determined through clinical trials. QIBA's Metrology Working Group has focused on technical performance, emphasizing that no measurement result is complete without an accompanying statement of uncertainty—a principle often neglected in imaging data reporting.

Sullivan highlighted that the most critical technical parameters for QIBs are bias, linearity, and precision. Precision encompasses both repeatability (under identical conditions) and reproducibility (under varying conditions including different locations, operators, or measuring systems). For clinical decision making, reproducibility proves most relevant, although the required magnitude varies significantly with intended clinical use.

Sullivan noted that despite technical feasibility, quantitative imaging faces significant adoption barriers. Clinical reluctance persists even for mature, reliable QIBs, primarily because few clinical treatment decisions are actually driven by quantitative imaging results. While numerous papers suggest potential QIB applications, long-term validation data remain scarce, making clinicians appropriately cautious.

Broader resistance to standardization compounds these challenges. Inertia maintains existing practices without compelling reasons for change. Some resistance reflects unwillingness to accept external directives, while skepticism questions whether standardization truly improves outcomes. Professional concerns about ownership and credit create additional barriers, compounded by insufficient education for both radiologists and treating physicians.

He argued that regulatory gaps further complicate implementation, including the absence of national accreditation or certification programs ensuring quantitative imaging quality. These multifaceted challenges highlight the value of comprehensive solutions addressing technical, educational, regulatory, and cultural dimensions of medical practice.

Sullivan's considerations for improving standardized quantitative imaging acceptance emphasize the importance of clear rationales based on published data or expert consensus where data are lacking. He stated that standards should reflect broad stakeholder input through open consensus processes and remain dynamic documents that undergo periodic revision and evolution.

He stated that the fundamental message emphasizes prioritizing and incentivizing reproducibility as essential for quantitative imaging success. Through rigorous attention to measurement precision and uncertainty quantification, quantitative imaging can fulfill its promise of transforming radiology from subjective interpretation to objective measurement, ultimately improving diagnostic accuracy and patient care outcomes.

Sullivan ended by remarking that this transformation likely involves sustained commitment to technical validation, clinical validation, education, and standardization efforts that address both the scientific and practical challenges facing quantitative imaging implementation in routine clinical practice.

CENTRALIZED IMAGING COLLABORATIONS FOR AI READINESS

Paul Kinahan, head of the Imaging Research Laboratory at the University of Washington Medical Center, spoke about the need for large amounts of well-curated data for use with AI algorithms and described one approach to collecting such data, which involves centralized imaging collaborations.

He began by noting that the Food and Drug Administration (FDA) has approved more than 1,000 AI algorithms for medical imaging and that more than three-quarters of those are for radiology uses. Why have so many imaging algorithms been developed and approved? One of the reasons, Kinahan said, is that AI has clearly demonstrated an ability to help in analyzing medical images. Another, he continued, is that there are established digital workflows and universal data formats—in particular, the Digital Imaging and Communications in Medicine (DICOM) standard for transfer and storage—for use with medical images, which generally are not present with EHRs and other forms of medical data.

However, for these AI algorithms to be as useful as possible, he continued, they require very large amounts of data—hundreds of thousands or even millions of images—for their development, training, and evaluation (Willemink et al., 2020). "Where are we going to get that?" he asked. It is hard, he said, because the types of data that are most useful for AI purposes are lacking—in particular, accessible, representative, and curated data. By "curated," he meant data with the appropriate information attached—their provenance, context, and so on.

Many data are potentially available, he said, but most of them are in isolated imaging systems. Kinahan remarked that this works well for local clinical needs—for the diagnostic tasks at hand—but problems arise when researchers try to collect large amounts of data and try to make sense out of all of the different types of data, formats, and error bars, which may or may not be reported. There are also many obstacles to getting clinicians to share their data and images. "Sometimes it is a lack of motivation, like, 'Why should we do this?'" Kinahan said. "Or even if we are inclined to do this, 'how are we going to pay for it?'" And privacy concerns add to the challenge. The result, he said, is that many of the algorithms being developed are based on limited datasets and sample sizes.

For researchers using these imaging algorithms, the limited data available on which to train them lead to less-than-ideal results, Kinahan said. Several researchers have analyzed these failures and the obstacles to creating AI models with clinical utility (e.g., Heaven, 2021; Roberts et al., 2021), and they have noted that several things went wrong.

Kinahan stated that one issue was the poor quality of the data. Among the factors contributing to the poor data quality are mislabeled data, multiple unknown sources, duplicate data, no traceability, limited quality control, and lack of external validation. Other issues behind the poor performance of the AI algorithms, Kinahan said, included a lack of valid ground truth, a lack of communications between AI experts and biomedical experts, and problems with how representative the data were of the populations of interest.

Some large datasets of images do exist, Kinahan said. He assembled a list of some of the largest that had a track record, including the name of the database, whether it is free or paid, what modalities are included, whether the images are from multiple institutions or a single one, and the number of exams. An exam can contain anywhere from one image to thousands of images, depending on what the exam was, he noted.

Kinahan offered a few additional details on some of these datasets. For example, he said that the Cancer Imaging Archive is, in his opinion, an exemplar of curated data. "However," he continued, "it is cancer-specific, so it does not have other diseases necessarily, although there may be some by happenstance." The National Lung Screening Trial is extremely valuable, he said, but it only has CT images. And at least three companies sell access to data from multiple institutions and multiple modalities. Finally, of particular interest is the Advanced Research Projects Agency for Health (ARPA-H) INDEX project, which is under development specifically to serve as a resource for developers of AI imaging tools. The images in these collections represent just a small fraction of the available images, Kinahan noted. In 2023, he said, more than 600 million medical imaging procedures were performed at more than 12,000 imaging centers in the United States.

Kinahan then provided some details on the Medical Imaging and Data Resource Center (MIDRC). It was funded by the National Institute of Biomedical Imaging and Bioengineering and now also ARPA-H in response to the COVID-19 pandemic and the resulting recognition of a lack of easily accessible and usable imaging data. Kinahan is one of the principal investigators for the project, which is hosted by the University of Chicago.

The intent behind the establishment of MIDRC was, he said, to have "a curated set of data with provenance that's available [so] you can get the general idea of the workflow." To date, MIDRC has ingested more than half a million exams, he said, but it takes time, effort, and resources to process those, so they are not yet halfway through. Currently, about 190,000 exams are available for free. The images are curated in such a way that users can select the cohorts they are interested in, and the tool, Data Explorer, exists to help select data.

Kinahan noted that 20 percent of the data on MIDRC are permanently sequestered and not available to the public. These data are kept separate to allow for the testing or evaluation of algorithms, potentially for submission to FDA or other purposes, he said. The sequestered data are representative of the various populations in the full dataset. Furthermore, MIDRC has developed methods so that if people run tests on data and then come back to rerun the tests, they do not get the same data. "It is a randomly sampled with replacement process to be a statistically valid approach," Kinahan said. This is only possible because of how the data are curated and maintained, he commented.

Unfortunately, MIDRC and the other centralized collections today do not, in general, provide enough data to support many of the potentially valuable AI applications, Kinahan said. He briefly described two other approaches that could provide larger amounts of data.

The first was indexing. This is when a platform points to data from other sources. MIDRC currently runs the Biomedical Data Fabric Imaging Hub, which indexes directly into the Cancer Imaging Archive data, the Stanford Center for Artificial Intelligence in Medicine & Imaging data, and NCI's imaging data commons, which already holds almost 600,000 exams.

The second approach he mentioned was federated data sharing. In a federated data sharing system, the data are kept in the local institutions where they were generated, such as hospitals, while centralized model development takes place in a hub. "You can take the algorithms to train them there and update your models there," Kinahan explained.

In closing, Kinahan offered several summary points: Centralized repositories are valuable, but more data would likely be beneficial. Options include centralized, indexed, federated, and hybrid repositories. Curation is a fundamental aspect, and that involves resources. And the sustainability of any approach is an key component.

DATA MANAGEMENT TOOLS AND STRATEGY FOR RESPONSIBLE IMAGING AI

Dan Marcus, director of the Computational Imaging Research Center at Washington University School of Medicine, spoke about data management tools and strategies for use with responsible imaging AI.

Marcus began with a quote from Nobel laureate Geoff Hinton. In 2017, Hinton declared, "I think that if you work as a radiologist, you're like Wile E. Coyote in the cartoon. You're already over the edge of the cliff, but you haven't yet looked down . . . It is just completely obvious that in 5 years, deep learning is going to do better than radiologists." While AI has indeed made remarkable progress—with deep learning outperforming radiologists on specific tasks and tools like TotalSegmentator segmenting hundreds of organs in minutes—significant challenges remain, Marcus said.

Marcus stated that despite the hype, substantial issues persist in imaging AI. A 2025 National Institute for Health and Care Excellence guidance stated that "more research is needed on the AI-derived software to analyze chest X-rays alongside clinician review" and warned that AI-derived software should not be used for clinical decision-making support, as some commercial software for identifying lung abnormalities could lead to missed lung cancers (NICE, 2025). Marcus discussed key challenges: insufficient evidence of effectiveness and reliability, insidious algorithmic bias, questions about model generalizability when deployed locally, and concerns about effects on radiologist behavior and workflow.

Over the past 20 years, Marcus has focused on how imaging informatics can address these issues through XNAT, an open-source data management platform. XNAT serves as a comprehensive solution for managing and organizing workflows—bringing data in from sources, moving them through controlled workflows, and eventually making them publicly available.

Marcus organized imaging data in XNAT using what he called "the feature stack"—a hierarchical structure with source data at the foundation, progressing upward through increasingly processed and detailed layers, culminating in biomarkers or phenotypes at the top.

Four primary sources provide the foundation: open data repositories (Cancer Imaging Archive, MIDRC, Hugging Face) that are typically free but have limited outcome information; commercial datasets from academic medical centers like Washington University in St. Louis's CuriMeta, which are costly but well validated; institutional data from hospital systems, which are often free but require institutional access; and federated data systems that manage privacy concerns while introducing new challenges in model development.

XNAT's Scout Data Explorer approaches data collection in a new way by indexing EHRs, picture archiving and communication systems, and pathology databases. A language vision model extracts features from both image pixels and radiology reports into a vector database, enabling natural language queries. As Marcus demonstrated, users can ask for "patients under 85 with lung cancer," receive 768 cases, and then refine to "cases with emphysema but excluding pneumonia"—with the system using both image pixels and dictated reports to find matching patients.

Understanding data quality is crucial, but Marcus emphasized that the goal is not about finding only high-quality data. Rather, the goal is characterizing quality well enough to understand any analysis or model's operating characteristics. XNAT deploys quality control tools like MRQy, which generates hundreds of metrics including signal-to-noise ratio and database variance. These containerized tools can run at scale, providing quality metrics on 50,000 exams quickly through user-friendly dashboards.

He then discussed data curation tasks—harmonization, labeling, annotation, sorting, and organizing—that typically consume 80 percent of graduate students' time, leaving only 20 percent for innovation. Marcus noted that AI can be used to help with many curation tasks. His team built models that automatically align scan acquisition types to standardized labeling schemes using both DICOM metadata and image pixels, transforming weeks of curation work into minutes. Another tool classifies individual tumors by organizing datasets by tumor type and providing detailed image analysis including tumor location.

Computed data encompass radiomic features extracted from images—intensity-based features, histogram-based features, and textures. Marcus noted that this allows for easier transfer of data in the form of spreadsheets instead of massive data files. However, these features are sensitive to underlying data distribution, making proper characterization of preceding layers important.

At the feature stack's apex are computed phenotypes—that is, biomarkers that align with actual disease attributes like molecular tumor characteristics. These represent the "end game" for many companies and laboratories. Marcus demonstrated this with glioma work, characterizing molecular biomarkers (genetic aberrations involving IDH1 and 1p/19q) status to provide prognostic and treatment information. His team built a complete proof of concept spanning from hospital system source data through quality assessment, feature extraction, and automated tumor segmentation to tumor classification—all integrated into XNAT's automated tooling.

Marcus closed by saying that many different approaches to AI exist, but all benefit from proper data characterization. Such characterization can be supported effectively through an informatics platform like XNAT. The platform transforms the traditionally labor-intensive, error-prone process of medical imaging data management into an automated, scalable system—enabling researchers to focus on innovation rather than data management. When a patient enters the system, the entire processing stream launches automatically, ending in patient classification and predictive insights that guide clinical decision making.

DISCUSSION

Chiang began by asking if the concepts discussed in the session—data quality, data quantity, metadata, data context, data management, and so on—are being taught to students in universities or if we have an education gap.

Sullivan noted that an education gap may exist for both the users and the radiologists. A lack of understanding may be present among many users—specifically referring physicians—that quantitative properties can be extracted from images: "They think of images as pictures, and they do not think of them as a source of quantitative metrics in the same way that they would think about getting lab tests on tissues or specimens."

Marcus answered that one of the biggest education issues is the gap between the people who build AI and the people who consume it. For instance, the backgrounds of graduate students in his laboratory tend to be in computer science or electrical engineering, rather than biology or biomedicine, so they often do not have a clear idea about a radiologist's workflow or even how to look at an MRI scan.

Chung said that there is a training gap. The people who know how to make the tools may not understand what tools are needed, while the people for whom the tools are designed may not know how to use them.

Kinahan described another type of gap. Radiologists and referring physicians are comfortable with the practice of referring a patient for a scan, the radiologist doing the scan and interpreting it, and then the referring physician getting the scan and the interpretation. "It is a system that works well," he said. However, he added, if the goal is also to use all those radiological data for other purposes, such as building AI models, "then there is a gap in the knowledge of what's needed for that, both in terms of the data integrity or curation as well as just how to manage large volumes."

Li asked how to prevent AI model outputs from being "garbage," given data quality issues, and whether AI could curate poor-quality data to "launder" them for training algorithms. Chung responded that the best approach is determining what question needs to be answered and finding appropriate source data with proper metadata, noting that, for example, EHR notes are clinicians' inferences and recollections, not raw data. Kinahan confirmed that using "helper AI" to curate large, complex datasets has become a well-accepted practice, while Sullivan emphasized that even poor-quality data can be valuable if used in proper context with known quality parameters. Chung added that when AI models underperform in real-world applications, it is often due to different data quality between training and deployment rather than model failure.

To end the discussion, Chiang asked about situations in which AI is used to create a dataset that will in turn be used to train an AI model: "How do we ensure that bias and error stop being propagated?" Kinahan replied, "That's where quality control comes in [to make] sure that you're not using the same AI to curate the data as you're going to [use to] train the data with." In general, he continued, the AI models mentioned in the discussion would be doing very different tasks.

REFERENCES

Chung, C., and D. A. Jaffray. 2021. Cancer needs a robust "metadata supply chain" to realize the promise of artificial intelligence. *Cancer Research* 81(23):5810–5812.

Heaven, W. D. 2021. Hundreds of AI tools have been built to catch COVID. None of them helped. *MIT Technology Review*, July 30. https://www.technologyreview.com/2021/07/30/1030329/machine-learning-ai-failed-covid-hospital-diagnosis-pandemic.

Herzog, R., D. R. Elgort, A. E. Flanders, and P. J. Moley. 2017. Variability in diagnostic error rates of 10 MRI centers performing lumbar spine MRI examinations on the same patient within a 3-week period. *Spine Journal* 17(4):554–561.

Keane, P. A., and E. J. Topol. 2018. With an eye to AI and autonomous diagnosis. *npj Digital Medicine* 1:40.

NICE (National Institute for Health and Care Excellence). 2025. *Artificial intelligence–derived software to analyse chest X-rays for suspected lung cancer in primary care referrals: Early value assessment*. NICE Guidance. https://www.nice.org.uk/guidance/hte12, last updated February 10, 2025.

Roberts, M., D. Driggs, M. Thorpe, J. Gilbey, M. Yeung, S. Ursprung, A. I. Aviles-Rivero, C. Etmann, C. McCague, L. Beer, J. R. Weil-McCall, Z. Teng, E. Gkrania-Klotsas, AIX-COVNET, J. H. F. Rudd, E. Sala, and C.-B. Schönlieb. 2021. Common pitfalls and recommendations for using machine learning to detect and prognosticate for COVID-19 using chest radiographs and CT scans. *Nature Machine Intelligence* 3:199–217.

Steinkamp, J., J. J. Kantrowitz, and S. Airan-Javia. 2022. Prevalence and sources of duplicate information in the electronic medical record. *JAMA Network Open* 5(9):e2233348.

Thrower, S. L., K. A. Al Feghali, D. Luo, I. Paddick, P. Hou, T. Briere, J. Li, M. F. McAleer, S. L. McGovern, K. D. Woodhouse, D. N. Yeboa, K. K. Brock, and C. Chung. 2021. The effect of slice thickness on contours of brain metastases for stereotactic radiosurgery. *Advances in Radiation Oncology* 6(4):100708.

Willemink, M. J., W. A. Koszek, C. Hardell, J. Wu, D. Fleischmann, H. Harvey, L. R. Folio, R. M. Summers, D. L. Rubin, and M. P. Lungren. 2020. Preparing medical imaging data for machine learning. *Radiology* 295(1):4–15.

5
Digital Twins

Caroline Chung, vice president and chief data and analytics officer, co-director of the Institute for Data Science and Oncology, and professor of radiation oncology and diagnostic imaging at the University of Texas MD Anderson Cancer Center; and Sylvain Costes, former National Aeronautics and Space Administration data officer for space, biological, and physical sciences, moderated a session devoted to understanding digital twins, their potential, and the challenges to reaching that potential. Four speakers offered presentations, followed by a discussion period.

DIGITAL TWINS AND ARTIFICIAL INTELLIGENCE FOR PRECISION MEDICINE

Jun Deng, professor of therapeutic radiology at the Yale School of Medicine, spoke about the use of digital twins and artificial intelligence (AI) in precision medicine.

Deng began by defining precision medicine as using information about a person's genes, proteins, environment, and lifestyle to prevent, diagnose, or treat disease—often described as targeting "the right patients with the right treatments at the right time." AI may be able to revolutionize precision medicine through early disease detection, real-time patient monitoring, drug target identification, causal gene identification, and management of phenotypic and genetic heterogeneity. Modern medicine, Deng emphasized, is increasingly becoming a science of information.

He continued that digital twins represent a paradigm shift in healthcare technology. Deng defined a digital twin as "a digital representation of a real-world physical system or process that serves as the effectively indistinguishable digital counterpart of the original for practical purposes such as simulation, integration, testing, monitoring, and maintenance." The critical aspect is real-time synchronization—that is, the physical and virtual systems are linked to exchange information continuously.

A 2024 National Academies report, *Foundational Research Gaps and Future Directions for Digital Twins*, illustrates how digital twins function in medicine (NASEM, 2024). Data collected from patients through imaging, laboratory tests, clinical assessments, tissue samples, and biosensors inform models that simulate what happens in the individual's body. The digital twin relies on both individual patient data and general models of human body operations, creating an ongoing cycle where predictions inform treatments and treatment results feed back into the digital twin. Deng argued that verification, validation, and uncertainty quantification (VVUQ), which is the systematic approach to ensure that computational models are mathematically correct, accurately represent real-world phenomena, and properly characterize confidence levels and potential errors in predictions, are essential components.

A digital twin transcends simple computational models or AI algorithms. While these technologies contribute to achieving digital twins, they do not constitute the totality. He noted that digital twins involve three components: a physical entity, a virtual replica, and a connection between the two. Deng stated that they should embody the "five I's": individualized, interconnected, interactive, informative, and impactful. He stated that, currently, the examples of healthcare applications include personalized medicine, clinical trials, biomarker and drug discovery, biomanufacturing, device design, surgical planning, hospital management, and personal wellness.

Digital twins in radiation oncology involve multimodal patient data, multiscale modeling, and high-performance computing. Benefits include enhanced ability to predict patient outcomes, optimize treatment plans, and develop innovative research tools. However, barriers include the need for centralized data commons, patient-specific data assembly, and multiscale modeling (Jensen and Deng, 2023).

Deng outlined five potential applications in radiation therapy: real-time monitoring and comprehensive analysis of cancer patients' health status; treatment plan optimization based on individual patient simulations considering anatomy, treatment history, toxicity, goals, and preferences; virtual clinical trials; predictive toxicity modeling; and proactive maintenance with automated quality assurance.

For building digital twins, Deng proposed a blueprint based on five questions: What are the goals? What level of complexity is needed? Are required data available or accessible? Can uncertainty be characterized? Does a proper mechanistic model exist?

Deng then described three specific applications his team developed. First, the team modeled time-series patient data on metabolic indices collected before, during, and after cancer treatment. Since differences in these time-series data correlate with treatment outcomes and quality of life, understanding temporal correlations enables prediction. This model (Hou et al., 2022) successfully predicted future metabolic indices, although noisy data affected forecasts. To address this, he said, the team worked in latent variable space rather than data space, creating latent ordinary differential equations to solve variable correlations over time before mapping back to data space, to achieve "much better prediction into the future."

Second, the team created patient-specific digital twins following virtual radiotherapy workflows, enabling tissue characterization, radiation therapy assessment and adaptation, and monitoring. With corresponding health prediction and treatment outcome trajectory models, physicians can present various options to patients for shared decision making. The team also developed whole-body, all-organ toxicity monitoring, with a prototype dashboard that warns of potential toxicity and prevents adverse effects.

Third, the team developed biology-guided radiotherapy using positron emission tomography (PET) monitoring. PET signals reflect tumor metabolic activity, and with multiple scans before and during treatment, they accumulate time-series data. By integrating mechanistic modeling with patient-specific longitudinal PET scans, the team created individualized digital twins to predict non-small-cell lung cancer responses to radiation therapy.

Deng discussed four fundamental challenges in developing individualized digital twins. Data acquisition, integration, standards, and quality pose difficulties for digital twins and AI applications. Creating effective multiscale modeling amid human biology's complexity proves challenging, he said, particularly at the microscopic level where "there are so many biological phenomena we do not know quite well." Ensuring responsible AI applications—fair, transparent, accountable, robust, safe, private, and secure—represents another hurdle. Finally, he stated, developing necessary computing infrastructure is important.

The overarching challenge in developing digital twins involves fusing multimodal data from functional and molecular imaging, radiomics, liquid biopsies, whole-slide pathology, genomic profiling, single-cell profiling, patient-derived cell assays, intravital imaging, fitness trackers, and implantable sensors. As Deng noted, "Each technology gives us new light on patient health state, but it is a challenge to coherently fuse them together."

Looking ahead, Deng envisions human digital twins becoming fully functional and autonomous, deployed as human digital agents serving as true health companions and safeguards. These agents could interact with humans in the physical world and with other agents virtually. "Imagine that millions of those digital twins interconnect, and they just automatically . . . try to do some new knowledge discovery and correlation," he said. "That would be very powerful."

In his final remarks, Deng noted that human digital twins hold tremendous potential in precision medicine. Success likely involves deep understanding of human biology, with multimodal data integration and multiscale modeling as key challenges to overcome. Cross-disciplinary collaborations will likely be important as well.

MULTISCALE DIGITAL TWINS FOR PERSONALIZED RADIOPHARMACEUTICAL THERAPY

Greeshma Agasthya, assistant professor in the Nuclear and Radiological Engineering and Medical Physics Program at the Georgia Institute of Technology, spoke about using multiscale digital twins to personalize radiopharmaceutical therapy (RPT).

Agasthya began by highlighting the transformative potential of RPT. "The big promise of RPT," she explained, "is that it can selectively target cancer cells while it spares the normal tissue." This selectivity is achieved by attaching radioisotopes to molecules that target specific proteins or ligands on cancer cell surfaces and then injecting the composite molecule into the bloodstream where radioisotopes concentrate around tumors.

She noted that despite Food and Drug Administration (FDA) approval for late-stage cancer treatment, current dosing remains largely uniform across patients, with only one drug—Xofigo—calibrated according to patient weight. This represents a gap between current practice and RPT's ultimate goal of personalized dosing to maximize cancer cell death while minimizing unwanted side effects.

To bridge this gap, Agasthya's group is developing multiscale human digital twins that operate across multiple biological scales simultaneously. The group begins with a whole-body digital twin encompassing all major organs and structures and then introduces digital twins of multicellular tumors to examine radiation effects on subcellular components within those tumors.

Agasthya stated that for RPT applications, digital twins possess four critical capabilities: tracking radioactivity across scales (since some radioactivity reaches off-target organs despite molecular targeting), estimating radiation dose across scales, simulating drug uptake, and predicting patient-specific outcomes.

The development process begins with Duke University's Center for Virtual Imaging Trials' virtual human population, created from computed tomography (CT) images. These images are manually segmented to create extended cardiac-torso phantoms—that is, replicas representing both human anatomy and physiology. "We can build these digital twins for any new patient that walks in," Agasthya explained, and by using CT images from different treatment time points, they create digital twins that evolve over time. The team layers additional complexity by incorporating organ-specific representations, tumor models, and even cellular DNA models to study how three-dimensional DNA conformation affects radiation therapy outcomes.

Agasthya illustrated the team's approach through a study of lutetium-PSMA (Prostate-Specific Membrane Antigen), an FDA-approved RPT that would be examined at unapproved doses. Starting with a male phantom (body mass index 24) and adding physiologically based pharmacokinetic models, the team determined time-dependent radioactivity concentrations in different organs, particularly peak concentration times. This analysis revealed when the agent would be most effective in target organs and least effective elsewhere, enabling estimation of maximum radiopharmaceutical impact timing.

Agasthya explained that once they determine cumulative organ dose, the team members simulate dose distribution to both targeted and surrounding organs, modeling vascular systems through computational fluid dynamics to examine radiopharmaceutical perfusion and achieve spatiotemporal distribution mapping. At intermediate scales, they use computational models to seed cancer and observe tumor growth or shrinkage responses to therapy, while at the smallest scale they examine DNA damage using Hi-C (genomic analysis technique) data on three-dimensional DNA structure to understand radiation-induced double-strand breaks. By integrating this multiscale approach, they calculate DNA damage, repair mechanics, and predict cell survival fractions for specific radiation doses at particular body positions.

Moving this technology into clinical practice faces multiple hurdles. First, accumulating sufficient information for treatment personalization proves challenging, particularly given RPT's relative novelty. Additionally, imaging typically occurs only at treatment initiation, not between radiation cycles, and treatment plans change only when clinically observable quantities like creatinine levels shift. While the team ultimately aims to extract more patient information, it currently works with available clinical trial data.

The multiscale nature creates numerous complexities, particularly in multiscale VVUQ. The team works to integrate across temporal and spatial scales while understanding interactions among radiation physics, human biology, and drug uptake biochemistry. Uncertainties at one scale propagate across others, compounding data requirements, computational costs, and patient variability challenges. To address these issues, the team is building cellular digital twins for comparison with live cell experiments to enable VVUQ. The team is also developing validation methods for double-strand breaks.

Future work for Agasthya's group includes developing patient- and disease-specific multiscale tumor modeling, which is currently lacking. "We are also building AI-driven surrogate models to reduce the computational complexity of these digital twins," Agasthya noted, while building toward virtual clinical trials of RPT.

Currently, she participates in an Oak Ridge National Laboratory study that created 491 virtual patients with 10,000 simulations of various CT protocols, generating 125 terabytes of data currently under analysis. This massive dataset represents the scale of computational resources for comprehensive multiscale digital twin development.

In her closing remarks, Agasthya stated how her work demonstrates the potential for multiscale digital twins to revolutionize RPT through personalized dosing. By bridging scales from whole-body physiology to DNA structure, these digital twins can optimize treatment efficacy while minimizing side effects. However, significant challenges remain in validation, computational complexity, and clinical integration before this technology can fulfill its transformative potential in cancer treatment.

CARDIAC DIGITAL TWINS: FROM THE ACADEMY TO THE CLINIC

Charles Taylor, director of the Center for Computational Medicine at the University of Texas at Austin, spoke about cardiac digital twins. In 2010 he started a company, HeartFlow, that was focused on the diagnosis of coronary artery disease. Much of his presentation focused on technologies offered by HeartFlow and his story of utilizing CT technology and images to develop this digital twin model.

Coronary artery disease, characterized by atherosclerotic plaque buildup in coronary arteries, represents one of the primary causes of heart disease. While progressive narrowing reduces blood supply to the myocardium and causes angina during exertion, heart attacks typically result from ruptured plaques that form blood clots and cut off myocardial blood supply.

Taylor highlighted the diagnostic difficulties plaguing coronary artery disease assessment. He gave the example that roughly 80 percent of emergency room patients with chest pain do not have coronary artery disease, and among those who do, distinguishing between mild-to-moderate disease (manageable with medical therapy) and severe cases (requiring interventions like stent implantation) remains challenging.

Traditional noninvasive functional tests provide no direct information about coronary artery blood flow or disease. Consequently, many patients with positive functional tests undergo invasive cardiac catheterization only to discover no significant disease, while serious cases are missed due to false negatives. The fundamental problem, Taylor explained, is that these tests do not directly visualize coronary arteries and cannot measure disease at earlier stages. Even with substantial plaque buildup, vessels adapt through compensatory remodeling, maintaining myocardial blood supply until plaque reaches advanced levels.

Current assessment involves cardiac catheterization with pressure wire insertion to measure downstream pressure divided by reference aortic pressure under stress conditions (typically adenosine-induced). This ratio, called fractional flow reserve (FFR), a diagnostic measurement used to assess the severity of narrowing in coronary arteries, guides treatment: values greater than 0.8 indicate medical management sufficiency, while values less than 0.75 require revascularization. However, these invasive tests reveal that 60 percent of patients lack obstructive coronary disease, he said.

Taylor's solution involved using FFR derived from CTs to build patient-specific coronary artery models to simulate blood flow and predict pressure losses, enabling physicians to "see" arterial conditions without invasive procedures. After years of development, this digital twin technology—FFRCT—now operates in approximately 1,300 U.S. hospitals.

The FFRCT process encompasses three steps: anatomic modeling, physiologic modeling, and functional assessment using computational fluid dynamics. The most challenging aspect involves obtaining precise anatomic representations from imaging data, as coronary artery disease reduces arterial diameter and calcium in plaques creates significant artifacts in CT scans.

To overcome imaging limitations, Taylor's team collected data from patients who underwent both invasive cardiac catheterization and CT scans, using these datasets to train algorithms that create clearer images from CT scans alone. The team developed a human-in-the-loop AI foundation combining deep learning algorithms with analyst review and correction of centerlines, boundaries, and other features. These corrections feed back into databases training next-generation algorithms, creating continuous improvement cycles that eventually enabled processing of cases human analysts could not interpret.

Feedback mechanisms further enhanced results. Data processing occurred centrally with reports sent back to clinicians, and any discordance between predicted results and measurements triggered investigation and adjustments. As Taylor noted, customer-reported false negative and false positive rates dropped steadily between 2018 and 2023.

The second step utilizes anatomic information plus form-function relationships to infer patient-specific physiology, customizing population-based physiology models for individual patients based on their anatomic data. Finally, computational fluid dynamics quantifies blood flow and pressure in the individual's digital twin, providing comprehensive flow and pressure data for the entire coronary tree.

FFRCT technology is being adopted clinically for more than 400,000 patients across 1,500 centers, including many top U.S. heart hospitals. The technology receives uniform payment coverage in the U.S. healthcare system, and England's National Health Service mandates its use.

Multiple studies have validated its diagnostic accuracy, establishing FFRCT as the most accurate noninvasive test for predicting FFR (Driessen et al., 2019; Okonogi et al., 2021). Some studies demonstrate that FFRCT can improve ischemia patient survival rates (Zellans et al., 2021). FFRCT also enables identification of chest pain patients who can defer cardiac catheterization safely and those most likely to benefit from revascularization. The technology serves dual purposes in clinical practice: routine patient assessment and catheterization laboratory prediction and treatment planning.

Taylor emphasized that FFRCT represents the successful transition of digital twins from academic research to clinical reality. This transformation demonstrates how sophisticated computational modeling, enhanced by

AI and human expertise, can address real-world diagnostic challenges while improving patient outcomes and healthcare efficiency.

The FFRCT story is an example of how digital twin technology has the potential to revolutionize medical practice. By creating patient-specific models that simulate physiological processes, clinicians can make more informed decisions without subjecting patients to unnecessary invasive procedures. The technology's widespread adoption and proven clinical benefits validate the concept that digital twins can bridge the gap between computational innovation and practical healthcare delivery.

Taylor ended by stating that his work demonstrates that successful medical digital twins include not just sophisticated algorithms but also robust validation processes, continuous improvement mechanisms, and seamless integration into existing clinical workflows.

DIGITAL TWINS FOR DISEASE MODELING AND DRUG DEVELOPMENT

Jon Walsh, co-founder and chief scientific officer at Unlearn, spoke about the application of digital twins to clinical trials. He began by noting that in high-energy physics, simulations are a valuable tool for making experiments more sensitive. Physicists simulate everything—the detectors, the background, and the experiment—because the experiments are very expensive and simulations are a way to get the most return from them.

Clinical trials represent an $80 billion-a-year industry with complexity rivaling high-energy physics experiments, making them prime candidates for simulation technology, he said. Walsh explained that most clinical trials for new drugs follow three phases: phase 1 tests safety, phase 2 evaluates efficacy, and phase 3 provides regulatory-grade evidence of safety and effectiveness.

The current standard approach uses randomized controlled trials (RCTs), where participants are randomly assigned to treatment or control groups. While RCTs are considered the gold standard for experimental evidence, they have significant inefficiencies. Patients with diseases enrolling in trials want treatment, not placebos, and the large number of concurrent RCTs with similar control groups creates waste.

Digital twins offer a solution by maximizing utility of RCT data. "We think about using digital twins as adding information about the participants who are already enrolled in a trial," Walsh explained. This approach helps researchers learn more without adding participants—or achieve the same insights with fewer participants. Digital twins bring lessons from previous clinical trials and observational studies into new trials while maintaining the current RCT's integrity.

In clinical trials, digital twins function as sophisticated predictive models. Using an example from an amyotrophic lateral sclerosis trial, Walsh described how a digital twin starts with clinical data from patients' baseline visits before patients receive the trial drug. The goal is to predict what will happen during the study. "This is a basic machine learning problem," he explained. "You have data about a patient's health. [They] can be complex. You want to build a probabilistic model of longitudinal health for patients with the disease, and then you want to make comprehensive probabilistic predictions of their future outcomes, and that's the digital twin." The twin can be personalized, with future data providing feedback to improve predictions. These predictions inform RCT decision making (Alam et al., 2024).

Building these models involves extensive data collection and curation—a resource- and time-intensive process. "If you do not get it right, then you have a lot of problems building good, robust models [and] you spend a lot of time doing harmonization across different data sources," Walsh emphasized. Sources include clinical trial data, observational data, and registry data.

After data preparation, models are trained using architectures designed for different disease progression patterns and then validated across multiple performance dimensions. The model's predictions use Markov processes with Monte Carlo sampling. "An individual patient's data [are] represented through many different sample draws of their future outcomes, and you can take the mean, the variance, [and] any other statistics you want," Walsh explained.

The most regulator-acceptable method for incorporating digital twins is covariate adjustment, which Walsh's company, Unlearn, has used extensively with clinical trial sponsors. In trials measuring cognitive test score changes, the digital twin predicts what the endpoint value would be for participants not receiving the drug. This prediction serves as a covariate in statistical adjustment.

Covariate adjustment incorporates pre-known participant data to reduce treatment effect estimate variance, providing more precise drug efficacy measurements. The digital twin's prediction represents expected standard-of-care outcomes, not drug treatment outcomes. Walsh described forecast control outcomes from digital twins as "super covariates" providing maximum analytical power increases. Both FDA and the European Medicines Agency support using digital twins for smaller, faster, more powerful RCTs.

Walsh presented a retrospective analysis of a phase 2 Alzheimer's drug trial with 453 participants with early Alzheimer's disease. The model trained on more than 8,500 participants from control arms of nearly 30 past clinical trials and observational studies covering mild cognitive impairment to severe Alzheimer's disease. The model incorporated approximately 60 variables including demographics, biomarkers, and baseline severity measures from cognitive and functional assessments.

Walsh continued, stating that results showed dramatic variance reductions compared to standard covariate analyses—10–15 percent increases in treatment effect estimate precision. While seemingly modest, digital twins explained up to 25 percent of total variance, representing significant improvement. This translates to either boosted study power with constant sample sizes or equivalent power with smaller samples.

He noted that the practical implications may be substantial. A standard phase 3 trial requiring 1,600 participants, 21 months enrollment, and more than $500 million could be reduced to 1,433 participants using digital twin variance reduction, saving 2 months enrollment time and $59 million total cost. Alternatively, maintaining participant numbers could significantly increase study power. This technology represents a paradigm shift toward more efficient clinical trial design, reducing costs and timeline while maintaining scientific rigor and regulatory acceptance.

DISCUSSION

Costes opened by noting that speakers had different definitions of digital twins; he favored Deng's version, which emphasized an interactive system with time dependence and critical interactive aspects. He then relayed a question from the audience about creating a generic digital twin for humans that could be built upon and individualized for various purposes, such as digital cohorts.

Deng responded that this should be possible, starting with a digital twin containing different organ pieces—heart, lungs, liver, and brain—each with minimum required data capable of running basic simulations. These organs could be combined to create a generic human digital twin and then calibrated using individual patient data to create personalized versions.

Taylor agreed that creating general representations is aspirational but acknowledged the complexity. He noted that most digital twins focus on individual organ systems, suggesting that coupling various organ digital twins would be a good starting point. However, he stressed building clinically useful systems rather than pursuing perfect models, warning against spending time on frameworks without clinical application. He estimated that a full human digital twin could be a 100-year project, suggesting focused efforts to achieve wins and learn system improvements.

Deng disagreed with the timeline, suggesting that 100 years was too long for a complete human digital twin. He emphasized the value of collaboration, with different groups building individual systems and finding integration methods. Agasthya agreed with Deng and stressed the importance of frameworks and standards enabling different groups to combine their work effectively.

Walsh viewed this as a core machine learning problem involving disparate data sources, contextualization, and predictions. He saw this as the most efficient pathway due to current investment in the area and progress in associative memory large language model approaches, although he agreed with Taylor about the 100-year timeline for complete systems.

Taylor argued for standardization, citing the Digital Imaging and Communications in Medicine standard's tremendous advances in image analysis. He noted the current moment as ideal for building standardized frameworks for data sharing, which does not currently exist in digital twins. Regarding cardiac modeling, he noted that while his presentation focused on coronary vascular systems, more sophisticated whole-heart models are possible and already being developed, although not in patient-specific manners. He estimated that several decades will pass before clinicians can build digital heart models using all available multimodal data sources.

Deng emphasized the value of cross-disciplinary collaboration, describing his consortium's diverse backgrounds, including clinicians. The consortium pursues two goals: developing a shared online platform repository for groups interested in digital twin development and determining data requirements for whole human models. He acknowledged that nobody knows the answer to data requirements, so they are gathering domain experts from academic and clinical sides to collectively understand minimum required data for human digital twins.

Responding to a question about incorporating dosimetry calculations into RPT, Agasthya acknowledged the controversy while outlining advantages and disadvantages. Advantages include potential patient benefits from slightly higher or lower doses than standard, such as giving higher doses to end treatment in 3 weeks instead of 6 weeks while achieving similar improvements. Disadvantages include potential over-optimization, causing detrimental effects to individuals. She emphasized that digital twins capable of predicting outcomes could enable prospective dose adjustments rather than retrospective responses to declining creatinine levels. Reliable predictions would be valuable for treatment planning.

When Costes asked about the likelihood of prospective dose shaping given strict radiotherapy protocols, Chung noted cultural resistance to protocol changes unless toxicity outcomes create concern. Agasthya agreed, explaining that standard doses are preferred for multiple reasons: manufacturer ease, simple logistics involving standard vials, and hesitancy to change doses without clinical trials proving effectiveness of alternative regimens. She suggested that even low-fidelity digital twins could provide valuable information to tailor clinical trials for testing different approaches rather than testing everything.

Walsh noted potential complications if digital twins became companion diagnostics; FDA could require model availability for any dosing decision, creating logistical challenges. Taylor agreed that this could limit drug adoption if digital twins became required diagnostics, making pharmaceutical companies reluctant to pursue such approaches. Chung said that in her experience, physician resistance seems to come from a lack of confidence and trust in new technology. Taylor agreed that building trust takes time and it can be lost quickly through single aberrant cases or adverse events. Walsh emphasized operationalization as vital and probably the biggest problem to solve. Despite developing mathematically optimal digital twins for clinical trials, he discovered that building trust, reducing risk, and demonstrating practical usability is a long process.

Chung asked about data availability challenges across different centers. Taylor confirmed this as an issue, noting highly variable data quality. Academic medical centers typically provide high-quality data, while resource-limited centers with less experience provide lower-quality data.

Quoting Stephan Achenbach, a leader in coronary CT angiography, Chung emphasized that enforcing image quality standards and rejecting low-quality cases was one of the field's best practices. She stressed the importance of enforcing best practices for input data, citing "garbage in, garbage out," and noted that building digital models involves consideration of input data quality, standardization, and validation measurement system quality.

Deng described particular difficulties collecting good multimodal data. Despite institutional review board approval for his Yale University study, he encounters significant resistance within the system for data access. He stated that tremendous amounts of collected data sit in individual silos or databases, making them difficult to access.

Chung ended the session by requesting final comments from each presenter. Walsh started by highlighting data standardization as important to unlocking digital twins' potential; he described multiscale systems needing application programming interfaces across scales to model and understand systems, particularly in trials.

Taylor agreed but cautioned against overhyping AI. Despite being a "huge AI believer" who has witnessed its power firsthand, he noted current over-exuberance and warned against similar treatment of digital twins. He suggested careful model-building work instead of making 5- to 10-year predictions that will almost certainly be wrong and emphasized hard standardization work, clinical integration, and modesty about capabilities and limitations.

Agasthya agreed with both, adding that developing models that can guide people in practical VVUQ methods acceptable for understanding digital twin outputs is important. Deng felt that data access and multiscale modeling are the most challenging aspects, particularly given limited knowledge about relevant biological phenomena at microscopic levels. He emphasized the value of reaching out to domain experts for collaborative approximation-building, using real-world data to benchmark digital twin models for improved accuracy and eventual patient treatment improvements through model predictions.

REFERENCES

Alam, N., J. Basilico, D. Bertolini, S. C. Chetty, H. D'Angelo, R. Douglas, C. K. Fisher, F. Fuller, M. Gomes, R. Gupta, A. Lang, A. Loukianov, R. Mak-McCully, C. Murray, H. Pham, S. Qiao, E. Ryapolova-Webb, A. Smith, D. Theoharatos, A. Tolwani, E. W. Tramel, A. Vidovszky, J. Viduya, and J. R. Walsh. 2024. Digital twin generators for disease modeling. *arXiv* 2405.01488v1 [cs.LG].

Driessen, R. S., I. Danad, W. J. Stuijfzand, P. G. Raijmakers, S. P. Schumacher, P. A. van Diemen, J. A. Leipsic, J. Knuuti, S. R. Underwood, P. M. van de Ven, A. C. van Rossum, C. A. Taylor, and P. Knaapen. 2019. Comparison of coronary computed tomography angiography, fractional flow reserve, and perfusion imaging for ischemia diagnosis. *Journal of the American College of Cardiology* 73(2):161–173.

Hou, J., J. Deng, C. Li, and Q. Wang. 2022. Tracing and forecasting metabolic indices of cancer patients using patient-specific deep learning models. *Journal of Personalized Medicine* 12(5):742.

Jensen, J., and J. Deng. 2023. Digital twins for radiation oncology. WWW '23 Companion: Companion Proceedings of the ACM Web Conference 2023, pp. 989–993. https://dl.acm.org/doi/10.1145/3543873.3587688.

NASEM (National Academies of Sciences, Engineering, and Medicine). 2024. *Foundational research gaps and future directions for digital twins*. Washington, DC: The National Academies Press.

Okonogi, T., T. Kawasaki, H. Koga, Y. Orita, K. Umeji, R. Fukuoka, K. Hirai, K. Haraguchi, K. Kajiyama, Y. Fukami, T. Soejima, H. Yamabe, and N. Koga. 2021. Comparison of diagnostic performance of fractional flow reserve derived from coronary computed tomographic angiography versus single-photon emission computed tomographic myocardial perfusion imaging. *American Journal of Cardiology* 159:36–43.

Zellans, E., G. Latkovskis, C. K. Zarins, I. Kumsars, S. Jegere, A. K. Krievina, R. Rumba, and D. Krievins. 2021. Three-year survival of critical limb-threatening ischemia patients with FFRCT-guided coronary revascularization following lower-extremity revascularization. *Journal of Critical Limb Ischemia* 1(4):E140–E147.

6
Multimodal Applications of Artificial Intelligence

Artificial intelligence (AI) is such a broadly useful tool that its potential in radiation oncology, medical diagnostics, and occupational and public safety can seem almost limitless—and daunting to consider. With so many potential uses, determining which are most likely to be beneficial in the near future and which are not quite ready for the real world can be difficult. This session's speakers took on the question of which potential applications of AI and machine learning (ML) seemed most likely to be providing value to these three areas in the near term to mid-term, with a particular emphasis on multimodal AI models.

FINDING USE CASES FOR MULTIMODAL AI IN RADIOLOGY

Nur Yildirim, assistant professor in the School of Data Science at the University of Virginia, described the results of a survey in which she asked radiologists and clinicians about how AI-based applications could most help them in their jobs.

Yildirim's team conducted comprehensive research to identify the most clinically relevant AI use cases for radiology, focusing specifically on vision language model applications. The study involved interviews with seven radiologists and clinicians, four brainstorming sessions, and follow-up interviews with five radiologists and eight clinicians to evaluate proposed use cases.

She stated that the typical radiology workflow begins when a referring clinician requests patient imaging. The radiologist's team generates the images, and the radiologist examines them, provides findings and impressions, and then sends a report back to the referring clinician to inform patient care and treatment decisions.

Yildirim's research showcases multiple key AI use cases for radiology practice. The first use case involves AI-generated draft reports from radiology images. Clinicians and radiologists viewed this as highly valuable, particularly for saving time on multi-slice images and examinations outside their specialty areas. One radiologist noted the challenge of reviewing unfamiliar imaging types: "I might be a seasoned reporter for lung or cardiac, but . . . we'll get a neck computed tomography (CT) image . . . it is extremely difficult."

For this use case to succeed, Yildirim noted that AI is expected to deliver near-perfect performance, with clinicians accepting only a 5–10 percent error rate for corrections. They prefer short, standardized reporting formats with bullet points rather than prose. She noted that the optimal approach would have AI handle the findings section while radiologists maintain control over impressions. When accessed by clinicians, it is helpful for reports to be clearly labeled as preliminary, with potential applications for triage to help clinicians escalate suspicious cases.

The second use case focuses on clinical decision-support tools. She stated that rather than generic chatbot interfaces, clinicians strongly prefer tool-based interactions due to time constraints. They want specific contextual information tied to individual cases rather than general medical knowledge. This involves integration of image data with electronic health records, patient-specific information rather than generic knowledge, and workflow-specific assistance with separate interfaces for different specialties.

The third use case addresses patient history summarization. Both clinicians and radiologists spend significant time reviewing patients' past images and reports to understand baseline conditions, changes over time, and current status. AI-powered summarization of a patient's historical radiology reports and images could provide brief highlights of key events and findings. One clinician noted that having a summary of preexisting conditions would save a lot of time.

Several critical implementation guidelines emerge from this research. The most useful applications may be task-specific rather than attempt to create one model for everything. Clinicians think in terms of specific tools for specific tasks, and their mental models may align with system functionality to build trust. AI outputs could be presented in forms that fit seamlessly into existing clinical workflows. If radiologists spend more time working with AI-generated reports than current methods, adoption will fail. Chatbots are not optimal for clinical environments, as clinicians prefer direct tool-based interactions that provide immediate actionable information.

Given the high failure rate of healthcare AI applications, Yildirim outlined four key risk mitigation strategies. First is involving clinicians throughout the entire development process, not just at the beginning or end. Second is carefully considering when, where, and how AI outputs are presented to ensure they align with clinical workflows and decision-making processes. Third is designing for entire healthcare teams rather than individual clinicians, considering how different roles interact and collaborate in patient care. Fourth is beginning with lower-risk applications that do not directly impact clinical decision making or patient care, such as information retrieval and presentation tools, before progressing to more critical applications.

The research team is developing a hyperlinked image-report dataset at the University of Virginia, which includes radiology reports, images, and links between them. This high-quality dataset will enable exploration of downstream AI applications and further research into practical implementations of the identified use cases.

The research emphasizes that successful AI implementation in radiology involves deep understanding of clinical workflows, specific rather than general solutions, and careful attention to how technology integrates with existing practices. Yildirim explained that the focus could be on augmenting rather than replacing clinical expertise, with particular attention to time-saving applications that enhance rather than complicate current workflows.

AI AND MULTIMODAL MODELING FOR LUNG CANCER TREATMENT

Jia Wu, associate professor in the Department of Thoracic/Head and Neck Medical Oncology at the MD Anderson Cancer Center, described stratifying lung cancer patients for immune checkpoint inhibitor therapy using radiomics applications in combination with omics data. He presented two case studies focused on lung cancer and then spoke about future directions for the field.

Wu's research focuses on advancing precision oncology through AI, addressing the fundamental challenge of delivering the right drug in the right dose to the right patient at the right time. Currently, while multiple treatment options exist for cancer patients, medical oncologists lack reliable methods to determine which patients would benefit most from specific therapies. His work demonstrates how AI can bridge this gap through sophisticated predictive modeling frameworks.

The challenge of treatment variability became apparent through two contradictory studies involving early-stage non-small-cell lung cancer patients. In one trial, patients treated with stereotactic ablative radiotherapy combined with immunotherapy showed improved outcomes compared to radiation therapy alone (Chang et al.,

2023). However, a similar trial using identical settings showed no improvement with the combined therapy. This discrepancy raised the critical question of why similar strategies work in some populations but not others, suggesting that patient selection may be the key factor determining treatment success.

To address this variability, Wu's team developed a comprehensive predictive modeling framework using patients' imaging data and clinical information. The process begins with radiomics processing and qualification, where researchers meticulously analyze pretreatment scans, segment tumors and blood vessels, and extract quantitative features from the tumor, background parenchymal tissue, and vascular structures. After incorporating standard clinical information such as age and gender, the team feeds these data into separate predictive models for radiation therapy alone and combined immunotherapy treatment.

The framework includes a sophisticated analysis approach involving counterfactual analysis, where patient treatments are hypothetically switched to calculate individualized treatment effects. This enables ML-guided patient stratification, which is then compared to random stratification to determine clinical benefits. The model successfully identified subgroups that did not benefit from adding immunotherapy and patients who received only radiation therapy but might have benefited from combined treatment.

Understanding model interpretability became crucial for clinical adoption. Wu's team collaborated extensively with clinicians to decode what the AI models were identifying, examining blood vessels, tumors, intensity patterns, and surrounding tumor areas. They employed Shapley value analysis to determine which individual features the AI model used for clinical stratification and how these features interconnected. Radiation oncologists were shown patient information and AI predictions to help them understand the model's decision-making process.

The second major application involved addressing medical oncology challenges in late-stage lung cancer treatment. Standard treatment for patients without driver gene mutations typically begins with immunotherapy, followed by additional therapies like chemotherapy. However, oncologists currently have no reliable indicators for selecting additional therapies or determining treatment duration. Wu's team approached this through a multicenter collaboration with Mayo Clinic, Stand Up To Cancer, and Dana Farber that examined patient data including genomic information accessible to any clinician, not next-generation sequencing data.

The research revealed important insights about model uncertainty and performance variability. When building and training five individual models, researchers found significant uncertainty associated with each model, and performance fluctuated when applied to different patient cohorts. Their solution involved quantifying uncertainty and incorporating it into predictions, which significantly improved model performance without requiring complex deep learning approaches. This highlighted the lesson that no model is perfect, and even small changes in optimizers or feature selectors can dramatically alter predictions.

Looking toward the future, Wu emphasized the need for integrated multimodal approaches to cancer treatment. The challenge lies in the vast amount of scattered cancer patient data across different systems, including radiology scans, digital pathology slides, molecular data, omics data, and clinical notes. The primary obstacle is that many of these data, particularly various images, lack structure, making meaningful feature extraction difficult and expensive. Because no agreement currently exists on how to represent image features in clinically interpretable ways, extensive annotation of pathology slides and other materials is required.

The integration process involves several steps: identifying correlations among different data modalities, aligning them appropriately, and integrating these diverse data streams into unified models for clinical applications. Wu demonstrated this concept through a study of stage 4 metastatic non-small-cell lung cancer patients, predicting immune checkpoint inhibitor therapy benefits using CT images, laboratory data, and clinical information without relying on standard clinicopathological markers.

The multimodal model provided additional information beyond benchmark models based on comprehensive radiology, pathology, and genomic information. While the deep learning model's predictions for overall survival and progression-free survival weren't quite as accurate as benchmark models individually, combining them significantly improved predictive performance and patient stratification capabilities.

Wu introduced the concept of "habitat imaging" to address tumor heterogeneity challenges. Cancer tumors contain subclones with varying aggressiveness and treatment resistance, potentially dominating treatment outcomes. His team developed methods to identify high-risk subregions using multimodal imaging by applying two-step clustering to align CT and positron emission spectroscopy (PET) data at the population level and then mapping clusters back to individual scans to create intratumor heterogeneity maps.

These habitat maps enable patient stratification into low-, medium-, and high-risk groups for cancer recurrence after surgery using pretreatment scans. Adding circulating tumor DNA data further increases prediction accuracy. The team also explored AI's potential to predict PET scans from CT scans; the team found that synthetic PET scans closely resembled actual scans, with experienced radiologists only distinguishing them by noting the synthetic versions' superior sharpness.

Beyond oncology, Wu's work extends to cardiovascular applications. Myocardial blood flow assessment typically involves expensive, complex cardiac PET scans that are difficult for patients to access. His team investigated whether electrocardiogram (EKG) data, which are cheaper and universally available, could predict myocardial blood flow using AI models. While some information remained uncaptured by EKG data, the approach offers a faster, more accessible alternative with reasonable accuracy.

He stated that additional applications include pathology data analysis for stratifying patient outcomes after immunotherapy and understanding lung adenocarcinoma precursors. The latter research identified TIM-3 as a potential target for preventing tumor progression, leading to a pioneering immunosuppression lung cancer trial. Early signals suggest that administering immunotherapy to precancerous conditions may intercept lung cancer development before it becomes invasive.

Wu ended his talk by emphasizing the potential of multimodal models incorporating medical histories, clinical notes, structural and functional images, genomics, proteomics, transcriptomics, and metabolomics. He feels that once researchers gain access to these diverse data sources and can apply meaningful analyses, they will be equipped to address clinical challenges and advance precision oncology toward the goal of personalized, optimized cancer treatment.

INTEGRATING MECHANISTIC AND ML MODELS TO ASSESS CAUSAL EFFECTS OF RADIOTHERAPY ON PATIENT OUTCOMES

Igor Shuryak, associate professor of radiation oncology at the Columbia University Irving Medical Center, spoke about enriching the linear quadratic model (which has been the basis of radiation oncology for many years) with omics data and using the techniques of ML to assess the effects of radiotherapy on patient outcomes.

Shuryak's research addresses a fundamental challenge in radiation biology and oncology by combining traditional mathematical modeling with modern ML approaches. Mathematical modeling in this field has a long history, exemplified by the linear quadratic model, and these models draw from diverse data sources including animal studies, in vitro experiments, and human clinical data. However, traditional models are inherently simple and cannot incorporate multiple relevant features such as patient demographics, treatment and disease details, omics data, and imaging information. ML models, while capable of integrating multiple features and modalities to generate accurate predictions, have a perceived mystery to them that makes result interpretation significantly more difficult than with simple mechanistic models.

The integration of these two approaches aims to create more accurate and interpretable models by injecting concepts from simple models, such as the biologically effective dose from the linear quadratic model, into ML frameworks as engineered features. This integration improves ML model interpretability and can guide clinically actionable insights. By incorporating mechanistic elements, ML models benefit from a broader knowledge base rather than relying solely on their training datasets.

Shuryak's specific example involves predicting outcomes for head and neck cancer using tabular clinical data, with plans to extend the work to multimodal analysis incorporating image data. The foundation for this work lies in decades of understanding about tumor repopulation, which has been recognized since the 1980s as a strong factor in radiotherapy outcomes for head and neck squamous cell carcinoma. Shortening radiotherapy course length helps reduce repopulation effects by limiting time for tumor cell proliferation, while treatment gaps have the opposite effect.

The Withers "hockey stick" model captures this phenomenon by assuming that accelerated repopulation begins at a fixed time point, typically 28 days after beginning radiotherapy, with a repopulation rate independent of cell-killing intensity (Withers et al., 1988). Shuryak refers to this as the dose-independent model. To improve biological plausibility while maintaining simplicity, his team hypothesized that repopulation might compensate for cell killing and suggested that more intense cell killing through larger doses could alter both repopulation onset time and rate. This led to development of a dose-dependent modification to test whether the model could predict population dynamics more accurately.

The team tested both models against various datasets, including older clinical trials and the comprehensive RADCURE dataset from Princess Margaret Hospital, which contains data on more than 2,600 head and neck cancer patients with detailed radiotherapy and chemotherapy information, clinical variables, and long-term mortality outcomes. This analysis employed a two-step approach that combined mechanistic modeling concepts with ML techniques, using random survival forests for exploratory analysis followed by causal survival forests for focused causal analysis (Shuryak et al., 2018, 2019, 2024).

Both dose-independent and dose-dependent models incorporate identical cell-killing terms from the linear quadratic model but differ in their repopulation terms. To maintain simplicity, the team made various assumptions and simplifications, resulting in models with only five easily interpretable parameters each. Using RADCURE data and simple Cox regression on biologically effective dose, calculations showed that the dose was a significant survival predictor in the dose-dependent model but not the dose-independent model. When applying the more complex random survival forest model, which is nonlinear and makes fewer assumptions, similar trends emerged, with higher biologically effective dose associated with reduced mortality in both models.

Detailed analysis revealed that several variables were more influential than biologically effective dose, including age, human papillomavirus status, and smoking, which all demonstrated much larger effects on outcomes. This finding led the team to employ causal ML approaches to examine how biologically effective dose and other factors affected outcomes.

Shuryak noted that while ML is commonly used for predictive tasks, causal ML techniques exist and are rapidly evolving because exploring causality is scientifically important. Causal approaches offer advantages over typical correlational ML for personalized medicine, particularly in studying heterogeneous treatment effects and how patient demographics and disease details modify treatment effects. Additionally, he said, causal effects translate better than correlations to other datasets where data distributions and correlation structures may differ, and causal ML can work with observational clinical data, which are much more widely available than randomized controlled trial data, to provide causal insights about treatment effects.

Shuryak then said that unlike predictive tasks that involve only inputs and outputs, causal tasks incorporate three variable types: inputs, treatments, and outputs. The main objective of causal ML is quantifying causal effects of treatments on outputs, which Shuryak describes as an inference problem where the structure is assumed known but effect strengths are unknown—distinguishing it from the much more difficult causal discovery problem.

He said that specific causal ML techniques include double-debiased ML, which is doubly robust and can provide reliable causal effect estimates if either the treatment or outcome model is correctly specified. This approach involves modeling the treatment, modeling the outcome, and building a third model to relate residuals from the first two models, with this relationship interpreted as the causal effect.

The causal forest technique, originally developed by Stanford economists and econometricians (Athey et al., 2019), applies to medical contexts as well. Like double-debiased ML, the key step involves calculating residuals. It uses a random forest–like approach to split data into small parts, estimating local treatment effects within each through residual-versus-residual regression. The causal survival forest variant handles survival data, which are particularly challenging due to censoring that affects many patients in medical datasets.

When Shuryak's group applied causal analyses to RADCURE data, the group found that under both dose-independent and dose-dependent conditions, high biologically effective dose increased patient-restricted mean survival times by 0.5 to 1.0 years and increased survival probability by 5–15 percent several years after treatment. Similar analysis of chemotherapy patients found that chemotherapy increased survival probability by 15 percent at both 3 and 5 years.

The team's next step involves incorporating image data into the analyses. The result demonstrates that combining mechanistic mathematical modeling concepts with predictive and causal ML models enables detection of biologically effective dose effects that align with current knowledge, although the chemotherapy effect was larger than previously published trials suggested. This approach has significant potential for enhancing knowledge about treatment effects from non-randomized clinical data to complement randomized controlled trial analyses, generate new hypotheses, and support personalized medicine development.

The work represents a promising direction for radiation oncology research, bridging the gap between traditional mechanistic understanding and modern computational capabilities. By maintaining interpretability while leveraging the power of ML to handle complex, multidimensional data, Shuryak suggested that this integrated approach could significantly advance personalized treatment strategies and improve patient outcomes in head and neck cancer and potentially other malignancies.

THE PROMISE AND CHALLENGE OF DEEP LEARNING IN RADIATION RISK ASSESSMENTS

Zhenqiu Liu, senior scientist at the Radiation Effects Research Foundation (RERF) in Japan, spoke about the promise and the challenge of deep learning in radiation risk assessment.

As background, Liu explained that exposure to ionizing radiation from natural and manmade sources is inevitable, making accurate risk assessment essential for radiation protection. While the risks of high-dose radiation are well established, the health risks of low-dose radiation—less than 100 milligray (mGy)—remain uncertain. Although some epidemiologic studies provide evidence about low-dose risks, the findings remain controversial.

He noted that traditional approaches to calculating excess relative risk (ERR) rely on nonlinear parametric (NLP) models with Poisson loss that account for factors such as sex, age, and location. These models have been the standard for radiation risk estimates for the past 40 to 50 years due to their simplicity and ease of interpretation. However, parametric radiation dose-response models face significant challenges. They have been criticized for inadequately addressing uncertainties in the low-dose range, and age-related modifications to radiation risk are typically constrained by specific functional forms.

To address these limitations, Liu described how researchers, like himself, have begun exploring deep learning applications in radiation risk assessment. Deep learning, also known as deep neural networks (DNNs), offers certain advantages including greater accuracy and flexibility, although these models are notably difficult to interpret. The integration of deep learning into risk models may resolve some current limitations of traditional approaches.

The three basic types of DNNs include feed-forward neural networks where information flows from input to output, recurrent neural networks that model sequential data ideal for time-series analysis, and convolutional neural networks that process spatial and temporal data used in image recognition. Neural networks are classified as "deep" when they contain multiple hidden layers, while those with only one hidden layer are termed "shallow."

Liu provided examples of recent research that has applied deep learning to improve radiation risk estimates, particularly for low-dose radiation exposure. One study utilized two large datasets based on atomic bomb survivor information: one containing solid tumor incidence data from 17,448 cases among 105,427 survivors (Preston et al., 2007) and another with leukemia data from 491 cases among 113,011 survivors (Hsu et al., 2013).

The research teams employed a DNN with three hidden layers to estimate radiation risk. DNNs offer several advantages over traditional models: They are data-driven and model-free, approximating underlying functions without encoding specific functional forms. They are also inherently nonlinear and do not rely on predefined parametric settings, allowing them to infer dose-response relationships directly from the data.

When comparing DNN performance with NLP models for solid tumor and leukemia incidence, the DNN performed comparably to the NLP in predicting leukemia incidence and somewhat better in predicting solid tumor incidence. However, the two models produced significantly different results for ERR despite very similar cancer incidence predictions. This finding suggests that accurate tumor incidence prediction does not guarantee precise radiation risk estimation, and since the actual ground truth remains unknown, determining which model provides superior ERR values is impossible. Similar differences between models were observed for ERR predictions at low doses.

To analyze and understand AI model predictions, researchers employed SHAP values (Shapley Additive Explanations). SHAP values decompose model predictions into additive contributions from different variables, providing clear measures of feature importance. While linear models assess variable importance through coefficient magnitude, SHAP values generalize this concept to any ML model, capturing both linear and nonlinear effects (Janzing et al., 2020; Lundberg and Lee, 2017).

Liu stated that an analysis of SHAP values for solid tumor rates and ERRs revealed notable differences between DNN and NLP models. For solid tumor ERRs, dose was by far the most important factor in the DNN, while age at exposure was most important in the NLP model (with dose ranking second). These differences reflect underlying model assumptions. The parametric model assumes that radiation affects tumor risk only through age and dose interactions, and that radiation risk depends on dose in linear or linear quadratic form while following exponential or power functions with age. In contrast, SHAP values for the DNN indicate that radiation contributes to tumor risk both independently and through interactions with baseline variables. After adjusting for baseline effects on tumor risk, the contribution of baseline variables to radiation-induced tumor risk becomes smaller, which aligns with intuitive expectations.

Liu noted several limitations in DNN adoption for radiation risk estimation. Identifying sources of baseline risk and effect modification in parametric models is challenging, raising questions about whether DNNs can automatically detect baseline risk and model effect modifications. Domain knowledge presents another challenge regarding whether modifications should be guided by radiation physics or biology. Balancing data-driven learning with domain expertise remains a key challenge. Additionally, deep learning models are intricate and less interpretable than NLP models, require substantial computing resources, and make confidence interval estimation difficult.

Estimating risks from low-dose radiation presents unique difficulties for several reasons. Liu outlined how tumor risks vary significantly among individuals, and radiation risks at low doses are likely heterogeneous. Standard parametric models struggle to detect statistically significant radiation risk at low doses. The research goal is to leverage DNN insights about individual risk heterogeneity to improve low-dose radiation risk assessment.

Liu discussed four candidate models that exist for evaluating ERRs as functions of low-dose exposure: supra-linear, linear no-threshold, threshold, and hormesis models, each with distinct advantages and disadvantages. Individual responses to radiation can be categorized into different groups. Tumor-sensitive individuals develop tumors and are influenced by various risk factors including radiation. Tumor-resistant individuals never develop tumors despite risk factor exposure. Some individuals may be tumor-sensitive but have not yet developed tumors. Tumor-sensitive individuals who have developed tumors are likely radiation-sensitive, while tumor-resistant individuals are likely radiation-resistant.

Since individuals with leukemia are likely more radiation-sensitive, researchers developed a zero-truncated Poisson model using only subjects with leukemia. This approach detected statistically significant coefficients and ERRs for exposures in the 30–80 mGy range. Similar analysis of solid tumors yielded statistically significant coefficients and ERRs for exposures in the 90–100 mGy range.

Liu believes that DNN models may provide new insights into radiation risk assessment, with SHAP values helping identify both radiation-sensitive and radiation-resistant population groups. Considering tumor heterogeneity could enhance low-dose radiation risk assessment for both leukemia and solid tumors, as dose-response relationships at low doses may vary significantly across different tumor types and individuals. Identifying radiation-sensitive groups using epidemiological data alone presents challenges, since tumor sensitivity does not always correlate with radiation sensitivity, and any existing low-dose threshold may vary by tumor type and individual characteristics. The integration of epidemiological data with insights from radiation biology and physics may improve identification of radiation-sensitive and radiation-resistant groups, with personalized radiation risk assessment holding significant promise for future field advancements.

DISCUSSION

The discussion was moderated by Anyi Li, chief of computer service at Memorial Sloan Kettering Cancer Center, and Ceferino Obcemea, program director of medical physics at the Radiation Research Program at the National Cancer Institute. Li opened the discussion by asking Yildirim about the difficulties of interviewing diverse potential users of AI technology with varying backgrounds and perspectives. Yildirim acknowledged the challenges but explained her approach: "You're just trying to get the initial reactions of people to understand the clinical utility and their sort of overall acceptance around the potential use case or an application." She emphasized that her preliminary study aimed to identify promising directions, noting the importance of including participants with varying AI familiarity levels to avoid bias.

Obcemea raised concerns about data quality in multimodal modeling, questioning whether acceptable data quality could be maintained across different institutions with varying resources. Wu responded that data quality issues are complex, particularly in medical applications. He explained that while clinicians ask how many data he needs, his answer of "millions, if possible" is met with skepticism. Additionally, evolving treatments create compatibility issues—datasets curated before immunotherapy existed may not reflect current practices. Shuryak added that his head and neck cancer dataset involved extensive manual curation despite being only several thousand cases. He noted that models trained on U.S. datasets do not translate well to European countries like Poland, possibly due to population differences in risk factors.

When Obcemea asked about the generalizability of models using historical data given changed treatment techniques since the 1980s, Shuryak replied that doses have remained relatively stable, making this less concerning for his work.

Addressing an audience question about labeling practices for multimodal data across various sources (radiology, pathology, genomics, etc.), Yildirim emphasized the importance of building tools with labeling in mind and ensuring clinician participation. She noted that current healthcare systems are often old enterprise platforms that do not facilitate easy labeling.

Wu stressed the value of letting experts do their work first, learning from their processes, and then potentially introducing helpful tools. He shared his experience hiring five foreign-trained radiologists to create what may be the world's largest set of annotated whole-body CT scans (5,000 cases over 5 years), noting that an average radiologist lacks time for such detailed annotation work. Shuryak agreed, emphasizing the need for adaptation to existing clinical workflows. Liu noted different challenges at RERF, where he works with historical data and focuses on standardizing formats and building databases to link data sources.

When asked about generating synthetic PET images from CT data, Wu acknowledged the difficulty in understanding how anatomic data can predict function. Despite publication challenges due to reviewer skepticism, he noted that "anyone can take the code from our GitHub and try it; we test it and we find out [that it is] surprisingly really something good." He suspects AI discovers hidden patterns, similar to radiomics predicting gene mutations from scans.

Wu's team is scaling up to collect roughly half a million PET/CT scans from about 50,000 patients at MD Anderson Cancer Center. His team plans to embed this in clinical practice, generating synthetic PET scans from existing CT scans and comparing them with actual PET results. Disagreements between synthetic and real scans might indicate biological differences or new phenotypes rather than model failures.

Radiologist Don Frush asked about responsibility assignment when AI causes adverse patient outcomes. Liu stated that while adverse events are "everyone's responsibility," ultimately doctors decide whether to use these technologies and would have to take responsibility for interpreting and conveying the result. Wu emphasized that AI tools aren't magic and can make erroneous predictions with incorrect uncertainty estimates. He advocated for keeping humans in the loop rather than moving to full autonomy; he warned that radiologists might become complacent after AI succeeds in many cases, leading to errors when they stop paying attention. Yildirim ended the session by stating that humans should always remain in the decision-making loop, as clinicians excel at decision making and knowing when something isn't right. She sees the real value of AI in its time savings and cognitive load reduction through tasks like "drafting initial findings" rather than in clinical decision making, leaving more time for clinicians to do what they do best.

REFERENCES

Athey, S., J. Tibshirani, and S. Wager. 2019. Generalized random forests. *Annals of Statistics* 47(2):1148–1178.

Chang, J. Y., S. H. Lin, W. Dong, Z. Liao, S. J. Gandhi, C. M. Gay, J. Zhang, S. G. Chun, Y. Y. Elamin, F. V. Fossella, G. Blumenschein, T. Cascone, X. Le, J. V. Pozadzides, A. Tsao, V. Verma, J. W. Welsh, A. B. Chen, M. Altan, R. J. Mehran, A. A. Vaporciyan, S. G. Swisher, P. A. Balter, J. Fujimoto, I. I. Wistuba, L. Feng, J. J. Lee, and J. V. Heymach. 2023. Stereotactic ablative radiotherapy with or without immunotherapy for early-stage or isolated lung parenchymal recurrent node-negative non-small-cell lung cancer: An open-label, randomised, phase 2 trial. *Lancet* 402(10405):871–881.

Hsu, W. L., D. L. Preston, M. Soda, H. Sugiyama, S. Funamoto, K. Kodama, A. Kimura, N. Kamada, H. Dohy, M. Tomonaga, M. Iwanaga, Y. Miyazaki, H. M. Cullings, A Suyama, K. Ozasa, R. E. Shore, and K. Mabuchi. 2013. The incidence of leukemia, lymphoma and multiple myeloma among atomic bomb survivors: 1950–2001. *Radiation Research* 179(3):361–382.

Janzing, D., L. Minorics, and P. Bloebaum. 2020. Feature relevance quantification in explainable AI: A causal problem. *Proceedings of the Twenty Third International Conference on Artificial Intelligence and Statistics* 108:2907–2916.

Lundberg, S. M., and S.-I. Lee. 2017. A unified approach to interpreting model predictions. Red Hook, NY: Curran Associates Inc.

Preston, D. L., E. Ron, S. Tokuoka, S. Funamoto, N. Nishi, M. Soda, K. Mabuchi, and K. Kodama. 2007. Solid cancer incidence in atomic bomb survivors: 1958–1998. *Radiation Research* 168(1):1–64.

Shuryak, I., E. J. Hall, and D. J. Brenner. 2018. Dose dependence of accelerated repopulation in head and neck cancer: Supporting evidence and clinical implications. *Radiotherapy & Oncology* 127(1):20–26.

Shuryak, I., E. J. Hall, and D. J. Brenner. 2019. Optimized hypofractionation can markedly improve tumor control and decrease late effects for head and neck cancer. *International Journal of Radiation Oncology, Biology, Physics* 104(2):272–278.

Shuryak, I., E. Wang, and D. J. Brenner. 2024. Understanding the impact of radiotherapy fractionation on overall survival in a large head and neck squamous cell carcinoma dataset: A comprehensive approach combining mechanistic and machine learning models. *Frontiers in Oncology* 14:1422211.

Withers, H. R., J. M. Taylor, and B. Maciejewski. 1988. The hazard of accelerated tumor clonogen repopulation during radiotherapy. *Acta Oncologica* 27(2):131–146.

7
Bias, Ethics, and Regulatory Issues

In a session moderated by Leo Chiang, senior research and development fellow at the Dow Chemical Company, and Sylvain Costes, former National Aeronautics and Space Administration data officer for space, biological, and physical sciences, four speakers discussed issues of bias, ethics, and regulation related to the use of artificial intelligence (AI) in radiation therapy, medical diagnostics, and occupational health and safety.

AI INTEGRATION IN NUCLEAR REGULATION: NUCLEAR REGULATORY COMMISSION PERSPECTIVES AND STRATEGIC APPROACHES

Matt Dennis, data scientist in the Nuclear Regulatory Commission's (NRC's) Office of Nuclear Regulatory Research, outlined the agency's comprehensive approach to AI integration.

Dennis started by discussing how the nuclear industry, traditionally characterized as slow to adopt new technologies, faces a unique paradox. Most U.S. nuclear power plants currently operate using 1960s and 1970s analog technology—complete with dials, gauges, and those distinctive green control rooms that defined the pre-digital age. He warned that the industry should not ignore AI's transformative potential.

The regulated entities under NRC oversight are eager to harness AI primarily for efficiency gains, seeing immense potential to make operations "better, faster, and cheaper." However, the NRC's fundamental principle remains unwavering: efficiency cannot come at the sacrifice of safety and security. This tension between innovation and caution defines the current regulatory landscape, where the nuclear industry must pivot more quickly than ever before while maintaining its exemplary safety record.

NRC's strategic response centers on enabling the safe and secure deployment of AI in the nuclear sector while promoting stakeholder engagement and encouraging research and development. This dual approach recognizes that the agency is attempting to simultaneously prepare to regulate AI applications and leverage AI to become more efficient regulators themselves.

Dennis noted that NRC performed a comprehensive analysis that identified eight potential gap categories where current regulations, originally written with human-centric operations in mind, may need to be adapted for AI applications. Two areas particularly relevant to radiation protection illustrate these challenges.

The first area Dennis raised is that radiation safety support programs traditionally rely on radiation safety officers, committees, and support staff who manually collect dosimetry data, develop reports, and submit documentation. The prospect of AI tools that could collect, report, predict, and manage entire radiation protection programs raises fundamental questions about how such systems would integrate with existing human-centric regulations and guidance.

Second, the gap analysis revealed concerns about training and human factors engineering, particularly regarding how operators should be trained to use AI aids and tools. This parallels challenges in medical imaging, where radiologists could learn to work with AI-generated reports while maintaining critical human oversight. The nuclear industry's commitment to keeping "humans in the loop" reflects a broader ethical imperative to ensure AI serves as a tool that enhances rather than replaces human judgment in safety-critical decisions.

The NRC's approach extends beyond isolated domestic efforts, emphasizing collaboration with federal counterparts, international partners, and professional organizations. The agency maintains memoranda of understanding with the Electric Power Research Institute and the Department of Energy, ensuring alignment with industry developments and research initiatives.

Internationally, the NRC collaborated with the Canadian Nuclear Safety Commission (CNSC) and the United Kingdom's Office for Nuclear Regulation to develop the "CANUKUS AI Principles," which mirror similar efforts by health regulators like the Food and Drug Administration (FDA), Health Canada, and the Medicines and Healthcare Products Regulatory Agency. These principles provide high-level consensus guidance that transcends specific applications while addressing the unique challenges of nuclear regulation (CNSC, U.K. Office for Nuclear Regulation, and U.S. Nuclear Regulatory Commission, 2024). The alignment with FDA's predetermined change control processes for AI-enabled medical devices demonstrates how nuclear regulation can adapt existing frameworks rather than creating entirely new regulatory structures.

This collaborative approach proves particularly valuable given the lag in professional standards development. Traditional standards organizations struggle to keep pace with AI's rapid evolution, creating a timing mismatch between technological capabilities and regulatory guidance. The NRC's proactive engagement with state counterparts through the Conference of Radiation Control Program Directors addresses this challenge, particularly for radioactive materials regulation, in which states play a primary role.

Dennis continued stating that the practical implementation of AI in nuclear applications presents both technical and organizational challenges. Given the industry's analog heritage, integrating AI tools involves significant infrastructure investments and cultural shifts. However, specific use cases demonstrate AI's transformative potential. Nondestructive examination of weld defects exemplifies this opportunity. Currently requiring human inspectors to analyze thousands of images, this task represents an ideal application for computer vision algorithms that could enhance both efficiency and accuracy.

The NRC's internal adoption strategy identified 61 potential use cases, with 36 showing clear AI application potential (NRC, 2024). These range from basic productivity tools like AI-assisted document writing to sophisticated predictive analytics for operational findings and experience analysis. This dual focus—regulating external AI applications while adopting AI internally—positions the NRC to understand the technology from both regulatory and user perspectives.

Looking forward, Dennis stated that the NRC faces the challenge of maintaining appropriate governance structures while ensuring regulatory staff possess the technical competence to review AI applications. The agency's annual public workshops and symposiums serve as critical touchpoints with industry, academia, and research institutions, fostering the collaborative environment necessary for responsible AI integration.

The NRC's approach to AI integration reflects a careful balance between innovation and responsibility. By maintaining safety and security as nonnegotiable principles while actively engaging with technological advancement, the agency positions itself to navigate the complex intersection of AI and nuclear regulation. Dennis stated that the success of this approach will depend on continued collaboration, adaptive regulation, and unwavering commitment to the public interest that defines nuclear regulatory oversight (NRC, 2023).

Dennis ended stating that as the nuclear industry prepares for a potential renaissance driven by AI's energy demands, the NRC's approach to AI integration could serve as a model for how regulatory agencies can embrace technological transformation while fulfilling their fundamental mission of protecting public health and safety.

ISSUES IN THE USE OF AI FOR BREAST CANCER SCREENING

Etta Pisano, chief research officer of the American College of Radiology, spoke about the use of AI for breast cancer screening, which could offer insights into the use of AI in other areas. She focused on what AI can do, how it is being evaluated, and how it should be evaluated.

Pisano began by talking about the fundamentals of breast cancer screening. Breast cancer screening in the United States follows a well-established protocol for asymptomatic women, with screening typically conducted annually or biennially starting around age 40 and frequency determined by individual risk factors. Pisano's presentation outlined how this process creates a complex cascade of medical decisions that presents both opportunities and challenges for AI integration.

She described how the current screening process reveals significant inefficiencies that could be addressed with AI intervention. Of all women screened, 7–15 percent are called back for additional workup, which includes extra mammography views, ultrasound, and magnetic resonance imaging. Of those recalled, only 8–10 percent ultimately receive biopsies, and of those biopsied, merely 20 percent have cancer—translating to only 5–10 cancer diagnoses per 1,000 women screened. Perhaps most concerning, approximately 40 percent of breast cancers identified through screening were actually visible in retrospect on earlier mammograms but were missed at the time of initial interpretation.

Pisano noted that this statistical reality underscores why breast cancer screening has become the most common type of AI-related radiology application submitted to FDA for review. The technology's primary goals focus on reducing false positives at both the callback and biopsy levels while simultaneously reducing false negatives to ensure that no woman returns with a cancer that was previously visible on mammography.

FDA's approach to evaluating AI technologies in breast cancer screening emphasizes multiple assessment criteria beyond traditional accuracy measures. Pisano stressed that while mortality outcomes represent the gold standard for technology evaluation—as demonstrated in the definitive screening mammography trials of the 1970s and 1980s—such comprehensive studies are no longer practical given ethical constraints around control groups and the extended time frames required.

Contemporary evaluation focuses on four key metrics: safety (i.e., primarily accuracy in terms of sensitivity, specificity, and overall performance), cost-effectiveness compared to standard approaches, patient convenience, and enhancement of radiologist performance. Notably, the fourth metric transcends simple accuracy measures, recognizing that AI's value lies not just in diagnostic precision but in workflow optimization and professional support.

As of January 2025, FDA had approved 46 AI breast-imaging products for sale in the United States, although federal law and regulations maintain the requirement for human oversight—autonomous AI remains prohibited. The regulatory framework categorizes AI applications into five broad claim categories, adapted from earlier computer-assisted diagnosis terminology: triage, detection/localization, diagnosis/characterization, combined detection and diagnosis, and acquisition/optimization.

She noted that FDA approval requires testing across three distinct categories, each with inherent limitations. Standalone performance testing, the most common and practical approach, evaluates AI models against historical cases with known outcomes. While useful for training algorithms and demonstrating performance equivalency or superiority to human readers, this method faces significant challenges regarding case characterization, population representativeness, and adequate sampling of diverse breast tissue densities and lesion types.

Reader studies represent the second category, involving human readers of varying skill levels who interpret case subsets both with and without AI assistance. These studies face their own limitations: small sample sizes (typically 16–20 readers) cannot represent the full spectrum of radiologist capabilities, artificial study environments may alter reader behavior, and cancer case enrichment creates unrealistic prevalence rates that may not reflect real-world performance.

Clinical trials, the third category, remain largely impractical in the current regulatory environment due to ethical constraints around control groups denied screening. While cancer registry studies can approximate randomized trial outcomes, they lack the causal reliability of controlled studies.

Pisano highlighted two instructive examples where FDA-approved technologies encountered real-world implementation challenges despite rigorous approval processes. The first involved radiological AI for large vessel occlusion detection, which was approved as a triage device but subsequently used off-label for diagnosis and detection in clinical practice. This usage expansion proved problematic when the software demonstrated missed posterior circulation thromboses, illustrating the risks of off-label application beyond approved indications.

The second example involved computer-assisted diagnosis products for digital breast cancer screening, which received insurance reimbursement based on promising reader study data that suggested dramatic performance improvements. However, a comprehensive analysis published 20 years post-adoption (Lehman et al., 2015) revealed no difference in actual patient outcomes within large registry populations, demonstrating the potential disconnect between controlled study results and real-world clinical impact. Pisano said that these cases underscore the fundamental challenge that "even despite preliminary evidence from reader studies, in real life there was no difference in patient outcomes." This highlights the inherent risks when clinical implementation occurs without comprehensive clinical trial validation.

Looking forward, Pisano suggested that real-world evidence might provide a pathway toward autonomous or semi-autonomous AI implementation in breast cancer screening. The current radiologist shortage—with approximately 10 available positions for every candidate—creates urgent pressure for AI solutions that can meaningfully reduce interpretation time, particularly for images deemed negative by AI algorithms.

Proposed implementation strategies involve installing AI algorithms that meet specific performance thresholds in standalone testing and then monitoring real-world radiologist performance through comparative studies. These might include dual-reader protocols comparing AI-assisted with unassisted interpretations, with patients retaining opt-out rights for AI applications.

Beyond screening applications, AI development focuses on short-term breast cancer risk assessment, potentially enabling more intensive screening protocols and risk-reduction pharmaceutical interventions for high-risk populations. Pisano predicted such tools would become available within 5 years. Additional applications include real-time image quality assessment by AI to alert technologists about inadequate images that require immediate retakes, same-visit workup protocols to reduce patient loss to follow-up, and direct-to-biopsy pathways for high-suspicion cases.

Pisano ended by noting significant international developments that may influence U.S. AI adoption. The European Union has advanced considerably ahead of the United States in implementing and testing AI for clinical practice. Most notably, the United Kingdom is funding a comprehensive breast cancer screening AI trial using cluster-randomization to evaluate AI as a second reader replacement, potentially eliminating the need for dual human interpretation that currently characterizes UK screening protocols.

These international initiatives may provide crucial real-world evidence that could inform future U.S. regulatory decisions and clinical implementation strategies, potentially accelerating the transition from current human-centric screening models to AI-augmented or AI-autonomous systems while maintaining patient safety and diagnostic accuracy.

ADDRESSING BIAS IN AI-DRIVEN MEDICAL IMAGING: PITFALLS AND BEST PRACTICES

Amber Simpson, Canada Research Chair in Biomedical Computing and Informatics at Queen's University, spoke about best practices and pitfalls in addressing bias in AI-driven medical imaging. She began by briefly describing her background working at and with several institutions: The Memorial Sloan Kettering Cancer Center, the Canadian Cancer Trials Group, the Ontario Health Data Platform, and the Imaging Data Commons at the National Cancer Institute. She is a classically trained computer scientist, but after working on various projects at these different institutions, she describes herself as a "data generalist."

Simpson discussed how imaging AI models hold transformative potential for healthcare, offering the promise of predictive and prognostic biomarkers that are quantitative, noninvasive, and cost-effective. Simpson's presentation, drawing from comprehensive research conducted with colleagues at Memorial Sloan Kettering Cancer Center (Moskowitz et al., 2022), illuminated both this tremendous potential and the critical challenge of embedded biases that can fundamentally skew model results. Her systematic analysis reveals that understanding sources of bias and implementing effective mitigation strategies represents one of the most crucial aspects of responsible AI development in medical imaging.

The significance of addressing these biases extends beyond academic concern—biased models can perpetuate healthcare disparities, lead to misdiagnosis, and ultimately compromise patient care. Simpson's work provides a comprehensive framework for identifying, understanding, and mitigating these biases across the entire AI development pipeline, from initial study design through final model deployment.

The architecture of research studies creates the first critical juncture where bias can infiltrate imaging AI models. Simpson identified four primary sources of study design bias that researchers should navigate carefully. Incorporation bias occurs when outcome measures rely on information from the predictors (data used to make predictions) themselves, creating a circular dependency that can artificially inflate model performance. Simpson's laboratory faces this challenge when predicting treatment response from computed tomography (CT) images, where response is measured by diameter changes of the treated medical condition that depend on post-treatment imaging. While acknowledging this limitation, she noted that such approaches often represent necessary compromises when gold standard measures like pathological assessment involve invasive procedures unavailable for all patients and researchers are forced to accept imaging as a "bronze standard."

Verification bias presents another significant challenge, arising when analyses include only cases where outcomes can be determined and creating a nonrepresentative subset of the target population. Simpson provided the example that this bias commonly manifests in studies that include only patients with biopsies, where biopsy decisions were based on imaging findings. Such selection creates a fundamental problem: It risks underestimating false negatives within the broader population while overestimating test sensitivity, potentially leading to overconfident model performance assessments.

Spectrum bias refers specifically to lack of diversity in disease severity or case types within the study population, significantly affecting diagnostic test performance across different clinical settings with varying patient populations. This bias frequently occurs when models are developed using only extreme cases—very sick or very healthy individuals—and is often driven by practical constraints such as expensive assays that limit focus to high-risk patients only.

Sampling bias, the fourth category, refers more broadly to who gets included in the study at all—it's about missing entire groups of people, regardless of disease status. This can result from access barriers that prevent certain patient populations from receiving complete follow-up imaging, creating systematic gaps in data representation that can fundamentally skew model development and validation.

The image acquisition process introduces multiple layers of potential bias that can significantly impact model performance and generalizability. Simpson demonstrated this challenge through a striking example: Two CT images were taken of the same patient just 10 days apart at Memorial Sloan Kettering Cancer Center and another institution using different protocols and dose reduction strategies. Despite both being portal venous phase CT scans, the images appeared dramatically different, illustrating how technical variations can introduce substantial bias into model training and testing.

To address these acquisition-related challenges, Simpson's team conducted a prospective scan-rescan study involving patients from Memorial Sloan Kettering Cancer Center and MD Anderson Cancer Center, focusing on liver parenchyma imaging. The team added a second portal venous phase scan, varying the timing by plus or minus 15 seconds from the standard protocol. This approach recognized that contrast fluid administration creates dynamic liver attenuation changes over time, with images taken at different time points showing distinct characteristics due to varying contrast uptake patterns. These temporal variations represent just one example of the numerous technical factors that can introduce statistical bias into prediction models.

Beyond technical considerations, data acquisition can embed social biases that reflect and perpetuate healthcare disparities. Simpson highlighted the problematic history of race-specific correction factors in medical measurements, particularly the race-adjusted estimated glomerular filtration rate (eGFR) calculations that influenced kidney transplant eligibility for Black patients. While such adjustments have been discontinued for eGFR calculations, the historical data containing these biased measurements remain embedded in medical records and research datasets (Tsai et al., 2021; Vyas et al., 2020). This creates ongoing challenges for researchers on how to handle and compensate for these biased historical data in current studies.

The preprocessing stage introduces additional variability that can significantly impact model performance and reproducibility. Different filtering approaches, threshold selections, and discretization methods can yield substantially different results, even when applied to identical source data. Simpson emphasized that image features can vary dramatically based on discretization strategies, whether using fixed bin widths or fixed numbers of bins. This variability underscores the critical importance of detailed methodological documentation, which enables other researchers to replicate work and understand potential sources of variation.

Operator variability represents another significant preprocessing concern, as human factors influence both manual and semi-automated measurements, particularly in crucial tasks like image segmentation. These variations can introduce systematic biases that propagate through the entire modeling pipeline, affecting final model performance and reliability.

Perhaps the most critical risk in prediction model building is overfitting, which Simpson described as a model "capturing spurious associations in the training data in addition to associations that would be replicated in similar datasets." To demonstrate the danger of overfitting, her team conducted experiments with publicly available imaging datasets and showed that essentially any data could be manipulated to support virtually any conclusion. This demonstration highlighted a fundamental principle: when datasets are sufficiently small relative to the number of variables being extracted, overfitting becomes inevitable, leading to models that can "predict anything" but generalize poorly. Even large datasets can quickly become effectively small when researchers ask highly specific questions, leading to the same overfitting problems (Chakraborty et al., 2024). This relationship among dataset size, question specificity, and model reliability represents a critical consideration in imaging AI development.

Simpson concluded her presentation with a pragmatic acknowledgment of data limitations and suggested balanced risk assessment. She emphasized that data are inherently "incorrect and biased," regardless of quantity, with uncertainty embedded throughout. However, she argued that extensive knowledge about statistical bias provides researchers with the tools necessary to address many of these problems effectively.

Crucially, Simpson highlighted that the risks of biased data should be weighed against the risks of inaction. Significant risks are associated with leaving data "locked up in repositories for no one to use," she noted, and substantial risks arise in avoiding AI altogether. This perspective reframes the bias challenge not as a reason to avoid AI development but recognizes the importance of thoughtful systematic approaches to bias identification and mitigation.

The key lies in implementing comprehensive bias mitigation strategies throughout the AI development lifecycle. This includes careful study design that acknowledges and accounts for potential biases, standardized data acquisition protocols that minimize technical variation, transparent preprocessing documentation that enables reproducibility, and robust model validation approaches that test performance across diverse populations and settings.

By embracing this systematic approach to bias identification and mitigation, the medical imaging community can harness AI's transformative potential while maintaining the rigorous standards necessary for responsible healthcare innovation. Simpson's framework provides a roadmap for navigating these challenges while ensuring that imaging AI models serve to enhance rather than compromise healthcare equity and quality.

SHORTCUTS CAUSING BIAS IN MEDICAL IMAGING

Judy Wawira Gichoya, associate professor in the Department of Radiology and Imaging Sciences at the Emory University School of Medicine, discussed the various ways that AI models can take "shortcuts" to get to an answer, how that can lead to bias in the models, and ways to overcome that bias. In her estimation, the presence of shortcut is the biggest hurdle that should be overcome for AI to be used regularly in medical imaging. "These shortcuts are everywhere," she said, and they will likely involve serious work to overcome.

Showing examples from Geirhos and colleagues (2020), Gichoya explained that shortcuts arise when AI models spot patterns for prediction but not for the right reasons. In one example, an AI model captioned a hilly terrain photo as containing grazing sheep when no sheep were present—the model made this "intelligent guess" because most similar training images contained grazing animals. In another medical example, an AI model examining lung images concluded that a patient had pneumonia not because of actual disease indicators, but because a radiographic marker showed the patient was from the intensive care unit, where pneumonia is common.

To illustrate how shortcuts develop, Gichoya described how a convolutional neural network (CNN) might confuse camels and cows. In datasets where cow images typically include grass backgrounds and camel images include sand backgrounds, the CNN might rely on background rather than animal features for classification. This becomes particularly problematic with limited datasets where background provides a strong signal, resulting in cows on sand being identified as camels and vice versa.

Gichoya discussed a 2018 study that examined CNN performance across three hospital systems—Mount Sinai Hospital, the National Institutes of Health (NIH) Clinical Center, and Indiana University Network (IU; Zech et al., 2018). Performance varied dramatically depending on training and testing data sources. Mount Sinai had 34.2 percent pneumonia prevalence versus 1.2 percent at the NIH Clinical Center and 1.0 percent at IU. Models trained on Mount Sinai performed well internally but generalized poorly to NIH and IU due in part to overfitting to high prevalence and hospital-specific features. CNNs frequently exploited shortcuts, such as hospital-specific artifacts, as proxies for disease prediction, and sometimes outperformed models trained to detect true pathology.This highlights the danger of "Frankenstein datasets"—that is, combining datasets without accounting for underlying characteristics. Gichoya emphasized the need to rethink dataset construction and testing, suggesting that even rural hospitals could contribute to AI testing with just 20 cases to identify model failures.

She went on to discuss how an AI model for COVID-19 prediction appeared accurate within their training hospitals but external validation revealed a significant drop in the model's predictive capabilities (DeGrave et al., 2021). However, that same the model could predict patient sex with nearly 100 percent accuracy from chest images alone from both internal and external datasets, demonstrating a case of shortcut learning where the algorithm had learned to identify sex-related imaging patterns from the training dataset. As Gichoya noted, "If your data encodes specific care characteristics, the model is going to still figure it out and use it."

Gichoya went on to provide a series of examples where AI models produced results from shortcuts. Research on hip fracture detection revealed models were good at predicting technical details like what type of X-ray machine was used (perfect accuracy) and hospital procedures, but when researchers removed these shortcuts by testing on more balanced patient groups, the model's ability to actually detect fractures dropped to essentially random guessing. This shows the AI was mainly learning to recognize hospital patterns and equipment differences rather than the bone fractures it was supposed to identify. (Badgeley et al., 2019). Gichoya highlighted this example to warn that high statistical scores (such as an Area Under the Curve of 0.99) may trigger error investigations rather than celebration.

Examining knee X-ray images, Gichoya and her students could predict hospital origin based on slight differences in metal rod placement—details radiologists would not notice (Hill et al., 2024).

She then discussed how foundation models suffer similar shortcomings. Deep learning models in chest radiography exhibited sex- and race-related bias across subgroups (Glocker et al., 2023). Vision language models in histopathology achieved near-perfect accuracy when text labels were accurate but performed randomly without labels and failed completely with misleading labels (Clusmann et al., 2024).

Addressing claims that shortcuts only affect poorly developed software, Gichoya described an experiment with FDA-approved commercial osteoarthritis assessment software (Lenskjold et al., 2024). When researchers flipped knee images so right knees appeared as left knees, the model produced different severity grades for identical anatomical structures, indicating reliance on position-based shortcuts rather than actual joint pathology. This occurs because training datasets encode real-world patterns—such as, right knees typically show more wear due to dominant leg usage—that models learn as predictive features.

Gichoya's team demonstrated that standard deep learning models can identify patient race from chest X-rays, CT images, and mammograms with high accuracy (Gichoya et al., 2022). After 3 years, the mechanism remains unknown and isn't explained by imaging-related race surrogates like body mass index or disease distribution. This racial inference capability could unpredictably bias AI interpretations.

She ended by stating that given AI's susceptibility to shortcuts, the field should fundamentally rethink dataset construction, especially for multimodal modeling. "We need to think about testing more than training," Gichoya emphasized, "because if foundation models that see more data are still susceptible to the same pitfalls, then we have to change something." The field could make model auditing easier and identify failure points systematically. Without addressing these challenges, she said that "AI is not going to work for anyone." She stated that the pervasive nature of shortcuts—from simple background associations to complex institutional patterns—demonstrates that robust AI involves not only better models but also fundamentally different approaches to data curation, testing, and validation across diverse real-world contexts.

DISCUSSION

The discussion session following the presentations on ethics was moderated by Chiang and Costes. Costes asked the panelists about classifying data by level, noting that at the National Aeronautics and Space Administration, people classified data into different levels—that is, raw data, processed data, and so on. He wanted to know how this level of classification might be helpful in medical imaging and nuclear regulation.

Simpson responded that raw CT images in sinogram space hold about 1 terabyte of data each, making them impossible for humans to interpret easily. "Those images are typically deleted from a CT scanner within a few days or a week because there just isn't space to store them," she said. This creates concern for doctors who want to see what they are working with, although attempts at using raw imaging data have proven challenging.

Pisano provided an example from a trial following 108,000 women at 133 sites worldwide, explaining different levels of evidence that a woman does not have breast cancer. A clean mammogram represents the highest level of evidence, followed by physical examination by a physician, then asking the woman directly, with the lowest level being absence from a cancer registry. She noted that unlike physics, where measurements and calculations provide comfortable truth, breast imaging has no absolute answers. Even a double mastectomy with pathology showing no cancer evidence isn't foolproof, she said, as "even the pathologist can miss things."

Dennis said nuclear plant regulation faces similar evidence-level issues. For weld inspections, debate continues over whether synthetic data generation and physics-based modeling suffice or if expensive experiments are needed. "My thought on this is for us in the nuclear industry, there is a graded approach of using different levels of data depend[ing] upon the risk profile that's being applied," he said. Gichoya agreed that thinking in terms of different data types or levels is useful, starting with CT scanner data but recognizing that anonymized data and public domain data represent different levels due to aggregation or metadata removal. Synthetic data and foundation models with embeddings create additional levels, introducing "this concept of models as a dataset," she explained.

Costes elaborated on his question by describing how his students sometimes autoscale microscopy images to see them better, which can be disastrous. When looking at DNA damage in cells where sometimes no damage exists, autoscaling brings up everything in the nucleus instead of maintaining consistent levels. This human-introduced bias, often unconscious, causes training failures. That is why microscopy researchers return to raw, untouched, full-bit-range images; "You never put any human interpretation in the image," he stressed.

Costes brought up classic COVID-19 cases in which AI studies mixed European and American image data. One country had many ventilator cases while the other didn't, with each image having different methods for labeling and for what case was captured in the image. "So the training was perfect," he said, "but it turns out that the training was on the label of the image, not the actual medical case." He shared lessons about poor training dataset design and the potential for explainable AI (XAI) to avoid such problems by explaining model classification methods.

Gichoya noted many examples of problems with "Frankenstein datasets," in which different datasets with varying characteristics are combined into large training datasets, making them challenging to curate and use downstream. However, she cautioned that XAI may not be the complete answer, referencing Jayashree Kalpathy-Cramer's work showing that "if you even change the order of how you bring the chest X-rays, the XAI is inconsistent."

Dennis said standards and guidance can help by increasing reproducibility. Unlike medical imaging, where radiologists vary in their image-taking approaches, the nuclear industry is highly regulated and prescriptive about protocols for examining welds with computer vision. "That does create a slightly cleaner dataset that is reproducible among a variety of applications and use cases," he said.

Pisano suggested that this explains why breast imaging has become an AI development target—it is the most standardized radiology field, with images used to look for just one disease. Reporting standards exist for breast imaging and are being developed for other body areas, with image acquisition becoming relatively standardized throughout radiology.

Chiang introduced responsibility and accountability questions: "When an AI model makes a significant mistake with a negative outcome to the patient, for example, who is responsible? Is it the AI model developer who may be introducing all the biases in the model, and therefore the model is not very useful, or is it the . . . human who makes the final decision, the doctor who makes the final decision . . . versus the software developer who actually launches software for the doctor to use?"

Gichoya distinguished between AI not working and AI being biased, where bias means "your AI does not work equally for everyone." When AI makes significant mistakes with humans in the loop, burden tends to fall on that person, particularly since medical practitioners can get malpractice insurance. She referenced FDA guidance warning that the agency cannot do all necessary testing to ensure AI model safety, which means that "healthcare institutions that are deploying these models should be assuming responsibility and governance to make sure that [they are] safe." Ultimately, responsibility still falls on the human in the loop.

When Simpson asked whether companies creating AI applications should be held accountable, Pisano mentioned companies willing to take liability for people whom AI labels as negative for a disorder. "But I'll just point out [that] if they take all the negatives, it is a completely different job for the radiologist," she said. "And it is going to be a much harder job because every case is something you have to scrutinize and decide what to do about [it]." Gichoya commented that radiologists become good at their job by learning negatives; she questioned what happens when they no longer have those to learn from.

Dennis said that from the NRC perspective, people and companies operating the technology are responsible entities even with AI use. Neither nuclear power nor medical imaging is ready for fully autonomous AI. "So, even with agentic AI," he said, "we're in this weird in-between where we still have to, for a lot of these safety critical applications, have a human who is double checking that."

Pisano responded that human-in-the-loop necessity depends on the task. Safety-critical nuclear tasks require human checking, but some medical tasks may not. She cited breast density rating on a four-point scale as an example where machine misclassification would not be catastrophic, indicating that "you could probably trust that task to a machine without terrible damage to patients."

Costes raised the question of whether fully autonomous AI systems might become viable, given the industry's push toward developing comprehensive safeguards. The panelists' responses revealed deep skepticism about replacing human expertise entirely. Gichoya steered the conversation away from autonomy altogether, arguing instead for a more nuanced approach that leverages human strengths while addressing human limitations. She pointed to cancer detection as an ideal example, where the real challenge lies in those ambiguous cases in which masses fall into gray areas between clearly benign and clearly malignant. Rather than building systems to replace radiologists, she suggested that developers would create more value by understanding how radiologists actually work and designing AI to complement their existing workflows.

Simpson reinforced this perspective by highlighting something that current AI simply cannot replicate—the intuitive pattern recognition that expert radiologists develop through years of practice. She described how highly trained specialists can spot subtle abnormalities that would escape both novice eyes and machine algorithms—a kind of professional intuition that emerges from deep experience and that remains uniquely human.

Dennis brought a regulatory perspective to the discussion, acknowledging that the nuclear industry does see opportunities for AI deployment, particularly in lower-risk applications. Even in more critical situations, he explained, AI could potentially operate within carefully designed safety frameworks, similar to how the industry already uses passive safety systems and redundant controls to maintain security even when primary systems fail.

Pisano switched to discussing the economic realities of AI development. While she agreed that starting with simpler applications made sense, she observed that such "low-hanging fruit does not attract the investment" that more ambitious projects do. Investors, she noted, tend to favor comprehensive solutions like tests that can detect all cancers rather than more modest innovations targeting specific types of cancer, even when the latter might be more technically feasible and clinically useful.

Gichoya expanded on this theme, cautioning against the assumption that every healthcare challenge requires a technological solution. She emphasized the importance of examining entire systems rather than focusing narrowly on what individual algorithms might accomplish and suggested that many improvements might come from better integration of existing tools rather than revolutionary new capabilities.

To end the discussion, the moderators turned to questions regarding training future workforces given AI's rapidly growing power. Simpson noted her computer science department's intense focus on training approaches since AI can now generate code and replace programmers. "What does AI mean now for every discipline?" she asked. "What does it mean to be literate in AI? And how do we take those tools and those thoughts across all of these disciplines?"

Dennis said even with AI, subject matter experts highly trained in specific areas remain necessary, with AI as a layered tool. Subject matter experts may benefit from questioning mindsets and familiarity with AI for comfortable AI usage. "I will say from my own experience at our agency in the past 3 years, people have gone from being naysayers of AI to wanting to adopt it to being more comfortable with it, so I think we're in a transition place," he said.

Simpson said current undergraduates and new graduate students are "built differently." They take many online courses, learn across various areas, and do not see traditional disciplines as discretely as previous generations. "They are just getting so much more integration across all of what were historically silos," she said, predicting that in 10 or 20 years, many disciplines will become "one big discipline because they've figured out what this has to look like."

REFERENCES

Badgeley, M. A., J. R. Zech, L. Oakden-Rayner, B. S. Glicksberg, M. Liu, W. Gale, M. V. McConnell, B. Percha, T. M. Snyder, and J. T. Dudley. 2019. Deep learning predicts hip fracture using confounding patient and healthcare variables. *npj Digital Medicine* 2:31.

Chakraborty, J., A. Midya, B. F. Kurland, M. L. Welch, M. Gonen, C. S. Moskowitz, and A. L. Simpson. 2024. Use of response permutation to measure an imaging dataset's susceptibility to overfitting by selected standard analysis pipelines. *Academic Radiology* 31(9):3590–3596.

Clusmann, J., S. Schulz, D. Ferber, I. Wiest, A. Fernandez, M. Eckstein, F. Lange, N. Reitsam, F. Kellers, M. Schmitt, P. Neidlinger, P.-H. Koop, C. Schneider, D. Truhn, W. Roth, M. Jesinghaus, J. Kather, and S. Foersch. 2024. A pen mark is all you need—Incidental prompt injection attacks on vision language models in real-life histopathology. *medRxiv.* https://doi.org/10.1101/2024.12.11.24318840.

CNSC (Canadian Nuclear Safety Commission), U.K. Office for Nuclear Regulation, and U.S. Nuclear Regulatory Commission. 2024. Considerations for developing artificial intelligence systems in nuclear applications. https://www.nrc.gov/docs/ML2424/ML24241A252.pdf.

DeGrave, A. J., J. D. Janizek, and S. I. Lee. 2021. AI for radiographic COVID-19 detection selects shortcuts over signal. *Nature Machine Intelligence* 3:610–619.

Geirhos, R., J. H. Jacobsen, C. Michaelis, R. Zemel, W. Brendel, M. Bethge, and F. A. Wichmann. 2020. Shortcut learning in deep neural networks. *Nature Machine Intelligence* 2:665–673.

Gichoya, J. W., I. Banerjee, A. R. Bhimireddy, J. L. Burns, L. A. Celi, L. C. Chen, R. Correa, N. Dullerud, M. Ghassemi, S. C. Huang, P. C. Kuo, M. P. Lungren, L. J. Palmer, B. J. Price, S. Purkayastha, A. T. Pyrros, L. Oakden-Rayner, C. Okechukwu, L. Seyyed-Kalantari, H. Trivedi, R. Wang, Z. Zaiman, and H. Zhang. 2022. AI recognition of patient race in medical imaging: A modelling study. *Lancet Digital Health* 4(6):e406–e414.

Glocker, B., C. Jones, M. Roschewitz, and S. Winzek. 2023. Risk of bias in chest radiography deep learning foundation models. *Radiology: Artificial Intelligence* 5(6):e230060.

Hill, B. G., F. L. Koback, and P. L. Schilling. 2024. The risk of shortcutting in deep learning algorithms for medical imaging research. *Science Reports* 14(1):29224.

Lehman, C. D., R. D. Wellman, D. S. Buist, K. Kerlikowske, A. N. Tosteson, D. L. Miglioretti, and the Breast Cancer Surveillance Consortium. 2015. Diagnostic accuracy of digital screening mammography with and without computer-aided detection. *JAMA Internal Medicine* 175(11):1828–1837.

Lenskjold, A., M. W. Brejnebøl, M. H. Rose, H. Gudbergsen, A. Chaudhari, A. Troelsen, A. Moller, J. U. Nybing, and M. Boesen. 2024. Artificial intelligence tools trained on human-labeled data reflect human biases: A case study in a large clinical consecutive knee osteoarthritis cohort. *Science Reports* 14(1):26782.

Moskowitz, C. S., M. L. Welch, M. A. Jacobs, B. F. Kurland, and A. L. Simpson. 2022. Radiomic analysis: Study design, statistical analysis, and other bias mitigation strategies. *Radiology* 304(2):265–273.

NRC (Nuclear Regulatory Commission). 2023. *Artificial intelligence strategic plan: Fiscal years 2023–2027*. NUREG-2261. Washington, DC: Nuclear Regulatory Commission. https://www.nrc.gov/reading-rm/doc-collections/nuregs/staff/sr2261/index.html.

NRC. 2024. Advancing the use of artificial intelligence at the U.S. Nuclear Regulatory Commission. SECY-2409935. https://www.nrc.gov/docs/ML2408/ML24086A002.pdf.

Pensado, O., P. LaPlante, M. Hartnett, and K. Holladay. 2024. Regulatory framework gap assessment for the use of artificial intelligence in nuclear applications. Southwest Research Institute paper prepared for the Office of Nuclear Regulatory Research, Nuclear Regulatory Commission. https://www.nrc.gov/docs/ML2429/ML24290A059.pdf.

Tsai, J. W., J. P. Cerdeña, W. C. Goedel, W. S. Asch, V. Grubbs, M. L. Mendu, and J. S. Kaufman. 2021. Evaluating the impact and rationale of race-specific estimations of kidney function: Estimations from U.S. NHANES, 2015–2018. *EClinicalMedicine* 42:101197.

Vyas, D. A., L. G. Eisenstein, and D. S. Jones. 2020. Hidden in plain sight—Reconsidering the use of race correction in clinical algorithms. *New England Journal of Medicine* 383(9):874–882.

Zech, J. R., M. A. Badgeley, M. Liu, A. B. Costa, J. J. Titano, and E. K. Oermann. 2018. Variable generalization performance of a deep learning model to detect pneumonia in chest radiographs: A cross-sectional study. *PLOS Medicine* 15(11):e1002683.

8
Trustworthiness and Transparency in Artificial Intelligence

This session focused on trustworthiness and transparency of artificial intelligence (AI) models examined from multiple angles. The session was moderated by Anyi Li, Memorial Sloan Kettering Cancer Center, and Ceferino Obcemea of the National Cancer Institute.

MACHINE LEARNING AND LOW-FIELD MAGNETIC RESONANCE IMAGING: UNLOCKING A NEW CLASS OF PORTABLE SCANNERS

Matthew Rosen, associate professor of radiology at Harvard Medical School, discussed how machine learning and (ML) AI enable new classes of imaging devices, specifically low-field magnetic resonance imaging (MRI). A key focus of his discussion was to address uncertainty quantification and trustworthiness in AI-driven MRI, including methods to parameterize reconstruction accuracy, assess model generalizability, and identify failure cases. He highlighted both the promise and the limitations of ML in portable MRI, as well as addressing challenges in robustness, interpretability, and clinical deployment.

Twenty years ago, Rosen built his first low-field MRI using a 6.5-millitesla electromagnetic scanner instead of the powerful superconducting magnetic scanners found in commercial MRI machines. His initial goal was creating an MRI scanner capable of imaging patients both standing up and lying down, driven by his and student Leo Tsai's interest in studying how gravity affects the heart–lung system. Later discussions with the Department of Defense revealed broader applications—the portable low-field MRI could be deployed on battlefields because its weak magnetic field would not tear shrapnel from soldiers' bodies.

Today, low-field MRI is gaining acceptance among clinicians and professional societies as a potentially valuable tool. Dependent on ML and AI, Rosen's work focuses on MRI applications that genuinely benefit from low-field operation.

Commercial MRI uses high-field superconducting magnets for good reason—this represents the most straightforward path to high-quality images. The magnetic moments of proton ions in water molecules, which MRI manipulates to create images, are vanishingly small. As Rosen noted, "The only thing you can do is turn up the magnetic field to make nice pictures."

However, Rosen and his students developed an alternative approach to improving low-field MRI images. They combined physics strategies—high-efficiency sampling strategies and low-noise detectors—to maximize the signal-to-noise ratio (SNR) in the detector and then applied computational strategies, including magnetic resonance fingerprinting and deep learning reconstruction, to extract more information from images. Deep learning strategies became essential to this process.

Eventually, Rosen's laboratory reached the Johnson noise limit on its detectors with maximally efficient signal acquisition strategies, making further signal improvement seem impossible. Postdoc Bo Zhu then asked, "Can we just somehow delete the noise?" This question launched Rosen and his team's work on noise reduction. When an MRI scans a brain or other body part, it acquires data that get "reconstructed" into clinically recognizable images through an inverse Fourier transform. Multiple reconstruction methods exist, but reconstructed images invariably contain noise that can make recognition difficult.

Rosen's team drew inspiration from biological vision systems. "Our biological neural networks have been trained since birth on what makes an image—edges, patterns, [and] texture—versus noise," he explained. Human perception refines through exposure to and training on stimuli (Sasaki et al., 2010), with this perceptual learning proving critical for robust performance in low SNR settings (Lu et al., 2011).

Building on this learning-to-recognize-images concept, Zhu and others (2018) developed AUTOMAP (Automated Transform by Manifold Approximation). "The idea is basically to learn to invert an arbitrary forward model," Rosen said, "and it does it by identifying sparsity in both domains—that is, the signal domain and the image domain—to improve SNR and accuracy."

Sparsity provides a way to separate signal from noise. Natural images have special structure, and high-dimensional data can be represented with fewer coefficients in sparse domains. While images are not sparse in the image domain or Fourier domain, they become sparse when transformed to domains like the wavelet domain. AUTOMAP operates between data-defined sparse domains, hallucinating images from learned sparse convolutional feature maps. He continued by explaining that AUTOMAP takes raw case-based data on one side and produces reconstructed images on the other side. Importantly, AUTOMAP-produced images have SNRs two to three times higher than conventional reconstructions.

When applied to noisy low-field MRI data, AUTOMAP boosts SNR by factors of 1.5 to 2.5, with greater boosts at lower SNRs (Koonjoo et al., 2021). The team discovered that AUTOMAP removed "zipper artifacts" (caused by scanner issues creating alternating white-to-black pixels) from images despite not being specifically trained for artifact removal.

Since this AI system learns reconstruction by seeing many examples and hallucinating final images, similar to other AI applications, concerns arise about potentially missing tumors. However, Rosen noted that the particular mathematical problem AUTOMAP solves during reconstruction "is particularly immune to this kind of issue."

A study found that low-field MRI augmented with "super-resolution" AI worked as well for segmentation as high-field MRI (Iglesias et al., 2023). While acknowledging that such images can have problems—one study showed the super-resolution low-field technique creating nonexistent pathology—Rosen cautioned about diagnostic use: "If you're trying to use these super-resolution images for diagnostic purposes, you had better be careful." However, he added, "these tools in fact have their place," as demonstrated by segmentation work. Success depends on careful task selection and result verification.

Rosen continued by highlighting the work by Sorby-Adams and colleagues (2024), which added super-resolution and quantitative morphological measurements at low field. Portable scanners placed in Massachusetts General Hospital's memory unit scanned patients brought in by caregivers who noticed cognitive impairment. Calculated brain volumes of hippocampal regions, ventricular regions, whole brain, and white matter hyperintensity lesions proved comparable between low-field scanners with super-resolution and high-field scanners.

In imaging, numerous methods exist for forward encoding objects. X-ray computed tomography typically uses centric or radial encoding, while MRI employs Cartesian, spiral, and radial encoding—methods chosen because of familiarity with Fourier transforms. But better approaches might exist. Since AUTOMAP can learn to convert arbitrary forward encoding, Rosen suggested it could develop new forward encodings for imaging applications. "Maybe we could change the world or cut scan time by 50 percent or better," he said.

Drawing inspiration from Google DeepMind's approach to teaching AI to play Tetris—not by teaching rules but by providing game scores and asking for maximization—Rosen's team applied model-free reinforcement learning to forward encoding used in MRI scanner image acquisition. The team built an MRI simulator with an AI agent tasked with comparing ground truth digital phantoms to their encoded and inverse-transformed results. This approach yielded interesting slice selection methods and led to experiments where AI algorithms designed new effective pulse sequences for nuclear magnetic resonance.

Rosen ended his talk stating that MRI is now clearly possible in the low-field, millitesla regime through combining physics, computation, and deep learning. AUTOMAP provides a unified reconstruction framework trained on forward models, learning to solve arbitrary inverse problems while boosting SNR and image quality. Super-resolution plus segmentation can provide accurate quantitative morphological measurements, and his group has developed AI-discovered pulse sequences for quantitative magnetic resonance.

BLOOD PRESSURE MODELING WITH PHYSICS-INFORMED NEURAL NETWORKS

Roozbeh Jafari, principal staff member in the Biotechnology and Human Systems Division at the Massachusetts Institute of Technology's Lincoln Laboratory, offered a case study of blood pressure modeling using physics-informed neural networks (PINNs) and ways to consider trustworthiness of the model.

He began by talking about digital twins, which are virtual representations of the human body or parts of it. They get information about the body through sensors and then model what is happening in the body with such things as ML algorithms. They can be used to predict what is going to happen. They are similar to simulations, Jafari said, but, unlike simulations, they have to remain tightly coupled with what they are representing through a steady flow of information.

Referring to the saying that "all models are wrong, but some are useful," Jafari shared the following key questions concerning a digital twin: "What level of granularity are we going to use? How are we going to construct the models? How do we make sure that our models are actionable? How can we make sure that the models provide trustworthy information to us?"

Jafari believes that the models used in digital twins should be built from images or other high-fidelity data. In building a model, Jafari said, one problem that often arises is that one can understand the physics of the model but cannot really estimate all the hidden parameters of the model. One approach is to use scientific machine learning (SciML), a type of ML that, instead of learning the patterns in data, learns the laws of physics. "Can I use SciML to serve as a proxy for this model?" he asked. "That's what this talk is going to explain."

By learning the rules of physics, SciML models have several advantages over the more typical AI that focuses on patterns in data, Jafari said. For one, they can make accurate predictions in situations where not enough data exist for standard AI models to do so. SciMLs establish physical consistency and constraint satisfaction in a model, making it possible to quantify uncertainties. Additionally, SciMLs are generally interpretable and explainable, and are often generalizable and robust. They also have various properties that make a model more trustworthy, such as helping with data quality and bias mitigation as well as domain-specific validation and benchmarking.

The premise of a PINN, which is a type of SciML, is that it incorporates physical laws in learning from data, Jafari said. Thus, unlike a convolutional neural network, when a PINN sets out to find the best curve that explains data, it also has the constraint that the curve is dictated to obey physical laws.

In the remainder of his talk, Jafari spoke about his team's work to develop a digital twin that captures blood flow and pressure in an individual. The system consists of a wearable sensor that captures blood flow–related data from an individual plus a PINN that is knowledgeable about various physics equations describing the flow of blood through the bloodstream. In particular, Jafari characterized his team's contributions as personalizing the model to better reflect the characteristics of different individuals, building interpretability into the model (and thus increasing its trustworthiness), and developing ways to determine uncertainty in the data and the model.

As context, Jafari said that blood pressure is the "Holy Grail in medicine." It is the most important metric that cardiologists use, he added, and it can provide important information about risks to cardiovascular health. Jafari then discussed some basic information about blood pressure, beginning with the fact that the heart pumps blood through the body at a particular rate and a particular volume per beat, called the stroke volume. The product of the rate and stroke volume is the cardiac output—or, in essence, the power of the heart.

Artery walls have a certain stiffness that determines how much resistance the arteries have to the blood pumped from the heart. The blood pressure is a function of this stiffness. Ideally, one would like to be able to measure the stiffness of the arterial wall directly, but in practice one measures blood pressure, which, when graphed over time, results in a waveform where the minimum is the diastolic blood pressure and the maximum is the systolic pressure. Measuring this waveform is challenging, Jafari said, but the waveform contains information that would be diagnostic.

The blood pressure waveform can be approximated by the so-called Windkessel model, which is similar to models of electric circuits where an artery's resistance to accepting blood correlated with electrical resistance and the artery's compliance correlated with electrical capacitance. Using the Windkessel model, one can write and solve equations representing blood flow for a general reference physiological system. However, for the model to be actionable, Jafari said, it needs to be personalized, with its parameters corresponding to the arterial features of a given individual.

Jafari's team uses two different variants of the Windkessel model to model blood pressure. The two-element model uses arterial compliance and peripheral resistance, while the three-element model adds characteristic impedance. Both models have equations that are essentially identical to the physics equations describing electrical flow in a circuit with capacitance, resistance, and, in the latter case, impedance.

To illustrate how his team uses the Windkessel model to set up a PINN, Jafari provided an example using the three-element model. The model applies the penalty function into the loss function and take into account some of the characteristics of the participants—age, sex, height, and weight. The loss function has two components, he said. One is related to the data, "because you're using data to train the network and you try to minimize the error," while the other part is related to the physics; "you optimize your neural net based on the objective function."

The data the team uses in the model are collected via bioimpedance, with four-point sensors the team has developed injecting current into the skin and measuring the impedance. This makes it possible to measure blood pressure not only in the arteries but also in the capillaries. To use the model with an individual, the team induces changes in blood pressure by having the person exercise, for instance, or putting a hand in an ice bucket to cause vasoconstriction. The team also continuously measures the person's overall blood pressure using a phenol press machine that gives continuous measurement.

To train and then test their PINN, the team members worked with systolic blood pressure, which, in the example Jafari showed, ranged from 100 to 140 as the person's blood pressure was manipulated. To train the model, they used only data when the blood pressure was relatively high (above around 125) or relatively low (below 110). "The assumption was that if the model learns the physics of it, it should do a good job for the middle, too, because it looked at the two extremes," Jafari explained. And the model did perform well when tested on data from the middle, having a smaller error than a standard convolutional neural network. "What is more important," Jafari added, "is that it works better for extreme conditions, and that's because we learned the physics of it."

In situations involving disorders, chronic stress, or injury, such as hemorrhaging from a combat injury, blood flow goes into a different mode. In the case of a wound, for instance, blood is lost and cardiac output goes down, but then the heart begins to compensate, blood vessels constrict, the heart rate increases, and blood pressure goes back up. And what really remains elevated is the peripheral resistance, Jafari said. "That's the metric that I want to measure," he said. "I do not want to measure blood pressure because blood pressure is not giving me causation; it is giving me correlation."

The approach that Jafari's team has developed makes it possible to measure such things as peripheral resistance and arterial compliance. "In terms of understanding the interpretation of this," he said, "you could look into things like the characteristic impedance with the blood pressure in the presence of a specific maneuver" such as applying cold or pain. "You would be able to characterize this," he asserted.

And the interesting part of this, Jafari added, is that when the model is working well, the confidence on the physics side is going to be higher, which provides an indication of the trustworthiness of the model. "We need more work to be done on this topic," he said, "but we are going in the direction of showing some of the confidence coming directly from the physics of the neural net."

In closing, Jafari listed several things that still need to be done. He would like to model the different sources of noise, such as noise in the bioimpedance, and to have a better understanding of the uncertainties associated with estimating the parameters and with the hemodynamics. He would also like the PINN to be more nonrestictive—for example, to figure out how the parameters change from beat to beat.

Then, offering some takeaway messages, he said that real-time updating of the virtual representation for the digital twin is a key feature of his work. Prediction is a critical feature for digital twin applications and real-time decision support. Traditional data-driven AI models struggle with extrapolation beyond observed data and may violate physical constraints. And SciML and PINNs play a critical role, ensuring that digital twins remain trustworthy, physically consistent, and data-efficient.

ASSESSING UNCERTAINTY IN INDOOR RADON EXPOSURE ESTIMATES: IMPLICATIONS FOR RADIATION EPIDEMIOLOGY

Heidi Hanson, senior scientist and group lead of biostatistics and biomedical informatics at Oak Ridge National Laboratory, discussed the sources of uncertainty in indoor radon exposure estimates and what that uncertainty means for radiation epidemiology. As context, she said that radon exposure is the second leading cause of lung cancer in the United States, but it is not factored into any recommendations for patients to undergo screening, in large part because it is so hard to measure exposure to radon.

In particular, she said, her focus would be on the data used to estimate indoor radon exposure as well as on feature engineering and how that might affect exposure estimates. Currently, she said, radon estimates are based mainly on the location of people's residences since much of an individual's radon exposure comes from radon gas leaking up from the ground into houses, with basements being the places with greatest radon levels. However, Hanson noted, information on radon levels within homes is not available across the entire United States, so developing models for estimating this residential exposure is necessary. Unfortunately, such models are based on data with a lot of error. "So, yes, I can do very cool things," she said. "I can do machine learning algorithms [and] I can get awesome answers, but are those awesome answers right?"

Hanson talked about two different datasets. One has point-level data for approximately 60,000 residences in the state of Utah. All of the measures are pre-mitigation—that is, before anything was done to lessen the amount of radon in the home—and they were all taken from the basement or bottom level. For this dataset, the data are considered point-level because the actual address where each test was taken is available.

The second dataset contains individual-level estimates with zip code for approximately 720,000 residents of Pennsylvania. These data are also pre-mitigation and taken from the basement or bottom level of a home. The main difference from the Utah dataset is that while the individual readings were taken from homes, only the zip codes are available (not the addresses for those homes). The fact that the exact point locations are not available leads to problems, Hanson said.

Several factors can lead to uncertainties in the modeling of radon exposure, Hanson said, including such familiar factors as temporal variation, spatial variation, and measurement variation. But, she continued, she focused on the choices that are made in geoprocessing the data for a model and how those choices lead to uncertainty as well.

In creating a prediction model, Hanson explained, one needs to use various sorts of data, such as soil concentrations of radon, information about housing characteristics, information about the water table, elevation, and so on. Unfortunately, she said, these data come in many different shapes and sizes: "So I have a really big problem stacking different polygons—not everything comes into the point location." To deal with that, people generally aggregate up to the lowest common unit. For instance, since the exposure estimates in Pennsylvania are available only at the zip code level, she would take all of the more detailed information and aggregate it to the zip code.

Using the Utah dataset to illustrate, Hanson began by explaining how she does spatial indexing. The dataset has point locations for every house with a radon measure, and those appear on a map as individual dots. However, she said, she does not have similar location information for all of her data, so to get her data to a common unit she overlays a hexagonal grid over the entire space. In that way, she said, "I can always use the lowest level of information that makes sense and tie everything to one of those hexes. . . . I'm scaling up and down depending on the dataset that I'm using, but these grids allow me to do this. So this is truly just a data engineering trick."

When it makes sense, Hanson continued, she can aggregate multiple hexagons getting values for the new combined hexagons by using weighted averages of the values of the individual hexagons. Such aggregation has various weaknesses, and Hanson described one technique—population masking—that can be used to mitigate some of those weaknesses. For example, she said, there are various places in Pennsylvania where no one lives, so no home radon test values are available in those areas. So if she wants to run an analysis comparing the characteristics of the soil—particularly the percent of clay—against home radon values, she does not want to include soil information for those areas where people do not live. The answer is to take the map of soil characteristics across Pennsylvania and then "population mask" it. "I mask out everything that has no possible chance that I'm going to get indoor home radon test value from that area," she said. "Because we use this spatial indexing, we can easily stack and get the information that we want across all the different layers that we're putting in."

Aggregating spatial data makes it impossible to see all of the heterogeneity in the data, Hanson noted, and it also hides some of the bias. For instance, in Salt Lake County, Utah, areas of lower socioeconomic status do not generally have many home radon detectors, so little or no data exist in these areas. More generally, she said, she knows her data have various issues that she may not be able to solve, but because she does not want that to stop her from learning more about her data and creating better models, she works with what she has. But to do that, she needs to characterize the uncertainty in the data, which she does with what she called a triangulation method. "I know there are things I'm not going to be able to correct," she said, "but I want to use multiple models so I can have an in-depth understanding of what I'm really looking at."

Her triangulation method involves looking at three things—the average model, the quantile regression, and a volatility model—and combining the results to get a better idea of what is happening in her data. She began by describing an average model at the zip code tabulation area (ZCTA) level, noting small differences between ZCTA and zip code that were not important for the discussion. Using the random forest method, she models the average radon concentration and then she models the volatility of the estimates, coming up with the permutation importance of the top 10 variables for the average model. Not surprisingly, the model feature that ranked highest in importance was the soil permeability.

Showing a map of Pennsylvania indicating the average radon levels and coefficient of variance of radon concentration by ZCTA, Hanson pointed out those areas with very high variance. If one only looked at average levels, one would miss some of the places with high levels of radon exposure in areas smaller than the ZCTA. "So, by averaging I really am missing some things in my data," she said. "That is concerning if I'm trying to come up with an estimate that I want to use for precision health."

Examining her variability model, Hanson then identified the importance of the top 10 variables in explaining the model's variability. This helps one predict where the most variation will take place. "This is important," she said, "because it can tell me what areas I should not trust when I'm looking at those average level predictions."

Then she noted that by using a quantile regression forest—so now predicting the distribution rather than just looking at the average—she gets even more and different insights into the data. One takeaway, she said, is one gets very different results when looking at the fiftieth than when looking at the average. "So when I want to know what somebody in a zip code has been exposed to and incorporate it into the clinic," she said, "I should be very cautious when there's a lot of variation in my data."

Moving on from discussing errors in concentration, Hanson briefly touched on errors in measuring exposure. No one spends all of his or her time at home in the basement, she noted, so getting a better idea of individuals' exposure based on their movements throughout the day is important. Her laboratory is working on some ways that agent-based models can be used to simulate this. "This just helps me understand the exposure part of this at a much more detailed level than residential location," she said.

AI-ENABLED HEALTHCARE SUPPLY CHAIN RESILIENCE AND RISK MANAGEMENT

Jie Yu, head of digital and data science product management at Johnson & Johnson, described his company's efforts to use AI in building a more resilient global healthcare supply chain. His talk addressed how his company has developed an AI model-based platform to quantify different types of healthcare supply chain risks and simulate various scenarios of risk propagation and impact throughout the entire supply chain network—from raw materials through intermediates to finished products.

Since the COVID–19 pandemic, Yu said, the healthcare sector and most other sectors have experienced many challenges in the global supply chain network. For instance, a study Johnson & Johnson did with the consulting firm KPMG found that more than 75 percent of global healthcare organizations report having experienced supply chain disruptions over the past few years. Furthermore, Johnson & Johnson has estimated that a global or regional supply chain disruption can cost a company of its size roughly $500 million to $1 billion. Yu described the global events contributing to supply chain disruptions over the past few years.

Thus, improving the global supply chain has become a priority at Johnson & Johnson, Yu said, and over the past few years the company has developed a cross-sector, cross-functional global initiative to try to build a more resilient supply chain through the use of digital, AI, and ML capabilities. To do that, Yu continued, the company is trying to build more dynamic, nimble, and digitized intelligent solutions to manage risk factors proactively that may affect the global healthcare supply chain system. Johnson & Johnson chose to take advantage of the current AI and ML technologies to build a system that can examine supply chain risk factors and vulnerabilities and make recommendations about how to mitigate those risks not only to the company's different business units but also to the upstream suppliers, vendors, and external manufacturers in its network.

He then detailed how Johnson & Johnson is doing this, beginning with getting a clear idea of exactly what risks the company might be facing in case of supply chain disruption. To do this, it looks at "adjusted value at risk," which Yu described as "a powerful measure of vulnerability at all levels—node, product, portfolio, [and] network." The adjusted value at risk can be thought of as the product of the residual risk exposure (i.e., the likelihood of something happening) and the value at risk. Each of these takes into account a variety of factors. For instance, to estimate the residual risk exposure, one looks at geographic factors such as global security and climate issues as well as supplier factors and factors internal to Johnson & Johnson. To calculate the value at risk, one considers the time to recover, the time to survive (essentially how long the inventory on hand would last in case of a disruption of supply chains), and the effect on sales. These two factors, the residual risk exposure and the value at risk, are multiplied to get the adjusted value at risk, which, Yu said, "is a quantitative measure of the vulnerability of your entire supply chain network."

Yu next described the digital platform that Johnson & Johnson has built in this initiative. It has three basic parts, he said. The first looks into value streams—essentially the materials from raw materials to finished goods and then on to the distribution network and the customers. These value streams are captured in digitally rendered maps, he said, "so we have all [those] structured and unstructured data to be able to use for the next level of AI and machine learning and data science modeling work."

The core part of the platform, Yu said, is a vulnerability detection technology that uses an AI and ML model to quantify the vulnerabilities. On top of that, he added, "we do different kinds of scenario simulations to simulate when different disruptive events occur and what kinds of consequences they might have." Finally, the company develops risk mitigation plans based on the different scenarios that have been simulated and develops prescriptions on which investments to prioritize and sequence.

Showing a complicated diagram of the architecture of the system Johnson & Johnson created to do this work, Yu offered a few high-level observations. Many different data types are incorporated, he said, including the company's internal data on manufacturing and operations, procurement, and so on. The company gets extensive market data from external vendors to get a macroeconomic view of the risks to the company from supply chain disruption, and it also looks at climate and environmental data regarding risk to the supply chain.

A graph database model is structured to mimic how the information in Johnson & Johnson's databases flows from raw materials to intermediates to finished products, and simulations are run on that graph database model. The simulations are designed to understand the risks of supply chain disruptions and to test various mitigation strategies. These simulations look for how to minimize the impact of any disruptions on the company's supply chain, both from suppliers and to customers.

In closing, Yu described Johnson & Johnson's innovation in moving from the traditional supply chain network analysis, which was done in a more manual and qualitative fashion, to a much more systematic and qualitative approach. This makes it possible, he said, to manage the different risks predictively and to design corresponding plans for how to mitigate those risks in a predictive and proactive manner. "And," he added, "the whole process is automated as well, with all the automated datalink and data pipelines to flow the data from one end to the other end."

He finished with a list of next steps for Johnson & Johnson. They are improving its technology in order to, for instance, have more automated scenario modeling and simulation, to develop and scale a resilience investment recommendation model, and to develop new dashboards and user interfaces. The company wants to build expertise in supply chain resilience by, for instance, creating a dedicated communication portal for training, awareness, and internal and external communications. And the company is working to integrate the various elements in the whole supply chain network to bring the individual components together so that the company can respond in a coordinated way to any future supply chain disruptions.

DISCUSSION

The discussion opened with Obcemea asking about uncertainty quantification in the models the speakers had presented, a question that revealed the complex nature of assessing AI reliability in medical applications. Rosen acknowledged that determining whether his low-power MRI was "good enough" for clinical practice fell outside his expertise, but he explained that his AUTOMAP reconstruction approach offered ways to parameterize accuracy using local Lipschitz uncertainty methods. He stated that his team had confidence in the reconstructions' accuracy regarding radiological concerns.

While his team's quantitative morphological analysis work remained too new for extensive uncertainty quantification studies, Rosen explained that the team could evaluate performance against ground truths. The data consistently aligned with these ground truths across the team's studies, though he acknowledged potential limitations: "If we have some very large clinical outlier, will it break? Maybe . . . . If someone had a massive surgical resection, will we get the wrong answer? Maybe. We haven't looked at those cases yet."

Rosen contextualized his work within broader healthcare challenges, pointing to new Alzheimer's drugs that showed promising results but required frequent MRI monitoring for side effects. The potential patient population for these drugs far exceeded global MRI capacity for monthly or bi-weekly screening, creating an ideal application for low-field MRI technology.

Jafari explained that uncertainty in his sensor and PINN blood pressure modeling could arise from multiple sources: data noise, missing data, or model inability to handle specific data types. Different approaches exist for addressing these issues, including examining noise in data sources through available models and analyzing latent space distributions in neural networks to identify unfamiliar or overly noisy distributions. His work's specific goal involved learning physics and physiology laws through hemodynamic monitoring data to understand blood pressure. When models deviated from expected patterns—whether due to model changes or data that no longer fit because of noise—this deviation helped identify uncertainty and establish appropriate limits.

The question of how to report uncertainty led Hanson to describe her work using large language models for near real-time disease classification in patients. Her team trained models not only to classify diseases but also to learn uncertainty, enabling predictions that specified what could be trusted versus what required manual review or questioning. She explained her approach as identifying "spaces where there should be more questions or maybe more experimentation on what's happening in the data."

Li raised an audience question about the biggest gaps in current regulatory frameworks related to AI uncertainty, prompting responses that highlighted the rapid pace of AI development and its regulatory challenges. Hanson expressed the difficulty of keeping pace with AI developments, noting that she lacked exact answers for necessary policy changes because "I can barely figure out what to do in my own group. Every day a new paper comes out, and every day I am already behind." She emphasized that not every new development represents genuine signal, with much being noise, leading to challenges in parsing "what is real, what's fake, what's shiny, [and] what's reasonable to do." Her practical approach focused on thoroughly vetting models before use, and she acknowledged that this represents a practitioner's reality not a direct policy answer.

Yu provided an industrial perspective, describing AI-related regulation as a hot topic in healthcare. While healthcare remains heavily regulated overall, AI technology regulation lags far behind actual field development. Johnson & Johnson's response involves understanding the global regulatory landscape, recognizing that each nation has different evolving approaches. The company heavily engages with government agencies and academia to offer its perspective and help shape policy development affecting its operations.

An audience member's question about verification and validation practices revealed different approaches across medical imaging, academic research, and industrial applications. Rosen explained that medical imaging is typically built upon currently accepted standards. Newer developments, like 256-channel head coils, demonstrated performance improvements over existing state-of-the-art systems. Reconstruction advances followed similar patterns, with Rosen citing compressed sensing as an example where claims of under-sampling by factors greater than one-half initially caused skepticism despite being theoretically sound. The Food and Drug Administration eventually approved compressed sensing after proper demonstration.

Jafari noted that classic validation involves repeating techniques with new participant groups, though this isn't always possible, particularly for academic work. He argued that verification and validation approaches should align with end applications and intended uses. For his blood pressure measurement work targeting hemorrhage detection, validation needed to mimic specific standards examining coronary cases, which required benchmarks that rigorously examined potential failure points. He suggested increased use of digital evaluations, comparing the approach to validating airplane chips through simulation rather than jumping directly to expensive randomized controlled trials. For image segmentation approaches, phantom testing could occur before reaching clinical trials, offering more efficient validation pathways.

Yu described his industrialized project's two-part validation approach: large-scale simulation for better metric understanding, followed by Monte Carlo simulation when calculating probabilistic information flow and propagation in suppression networks. This helped his group understand how metrics matched across different scenarios the group attempted to mimic. His team implemented real-time or near real-time monitoring by building pipelines that incorporated external risk event data from third parties into their internal systems. This enabled near real-time calculation of events as they occurred, with back-validation to assess whether metrics provided reasonable recommendations for different scenarios.

REFERENCES

Iglesias, J. E., R. Schleicher, S. Laguna, B. Billot, P. Schaefer, B. McKaig, J. N. Goldstein, K. N. Sheth, M. S. Rosen, and W. T. Kimberly. 2023. Quantitative brain morphometry of portable low-field-strength MRI using super-resolution machine learning. *Radiology* 306(3):e220522.

Koonjoo, N., B. Zhu, G. C. Bagnall, D. Bhutto, and M. S. Rosen. 2021. Boosting the signal-to-noise of low-field MRI with deep learning image reconstruction. *Science Reports* 11(1):8248.

Lu, Z.-L., T. Hua, C.-B. Huang, Y. Zhou, and B. A. Dosher. 2011. Visual perceptual learning. *Neurobiology of Learning and Memory* 95:145–151.

Sasaki, Y., J. E. Nanez, and T. Watanabe. 2010. Advances in visual perceptual learning and plasticity. *Nature Reviews Neuroscience* 11(1):53–60.

Sorby-Adams, A. J., J. Guo, P. Laso, J. E. Kirsch, J. Zabinska, A.-L. Garcia Guarniz, P. W. Schaefer, S. Payabvash, A. de Havenon, M. S. Rosen, K. N. Sheth, T. Gomez-Isla, J. E. Iglesias, and W. T. Kimberly. 2024. Portable, low-field magnetic resonance imaging for evaluation of Alzheimer's disease. *Nature Communications* 15:10488.

Zhu, B., J. Z. Liu, S. F. Cauley, B. R. Rosen, and M. S. Rosen. 2018. Image reconstruction by domain-transform manifold learning. *Nature* 555(7697):487–492.

9
Final Remarks

Shaheen Dewji, assistant professor in the Nuclear and Radiological Engineering and Medical Physics Program at the Georgia Institute of Technology, offered a few concluding remarks in the symposium's final session. "Throughout the past couple of days," she said, "we've seen how AI [artificial intelligence] is reshaping medicine and public health, and we've also recognized the hurdles that still remain, whether [those are] in data governance, regulatory frameworks, or ethical considerations." Several key themes emerged from the symposium, she said, and she listed five of them using the "Wouldn't it be cool if . . . " phrasing introduced earlier by Heidi Hanson during her presentation "Computational Approaches to Integrating Radiation Exposure Across the Lifecourse: Risks, Insights, and Innovations" (Chapter 3).

The first theme was the use of AI in medical imaging and diagnostics. Symposium speakers described how AI is pushing the limits of medical imaging, improving resolution, reducing noise, and driving new standards for accuracy. She asked, but "wouldn't it be cool if we could fully automate imaging workflows without sacrificing clinician oversight or patient trust?"

The second theme was the use personalized medicine and digital twins. AI-powered models are paving the way for precision medicine, she said, and allowing clinicians to tailor treatment plans to individuals in ways never before possible. "So, wouldn't it be cool," she continued, "if digital twins could anticipate a patient's response to treatment before it even begins, reducing trial and error in clinical decision making?"

The third theme was the use of AI in radiation therapy and oncology. AI is changing the way clinicians approach cancer treatment through an integration of radiomics, genomics, and clinical data to optimize outcomes, but, she asked, "wouldn't it be cool if AI could dynamically adjust radiation doses in real time based on a tumor's immediate response?"

The fourth theme was data governance and ethical considerations. The power of AI is only as strong as the data behind it, Dewji said. Currently, she continued, issues of bias, access, and standardization stand in the way of equitable AI deployment, "but wouldn't it be cool if we could create fully interoperable bias-free datasets that fuel AI models without compromising privacy?"

And the fifth theme was the use of AI for risk management and public safety. From exposure modeling to emergency preparedness, she said, AI is proving to be an essential tool in radiation protection, but "wouldn't it be cool if AI could predict not just the risks we know but also the ones we haven't yet imagined?"

Looking ahead, she continued, the power of AI lies not just in what it can do today but also in how people choose to develop, refine, and deploy it responsibly for the future. First, "to make the most of these innovations," she said, "we need to first ensure that there is trustworthy AI, ensuring the models are transparent, explainable, and clinically validated." This builds on earlier discussions where symposium participants highlighted the importance of integrating data labeling into workflows, using clinical settings as a key example. This approach could ensure that researchers and clinicians maintain human-driven feedback loops in their work to enhance the relevance, precision, and generalizability of AI models over time. Second, regulatory alignment —integrating AI into medicine and public health while maintaining rigorous safety standards. And third, multidisciplinary collaboration will be crucial to the ongoing health of the field, with people from diverse disciplines and sectors looking at fostering partnerships, including new partnerships across research, industry, and policy, to create AI that is safe, effective, and equitable. This connects to a key theme mentioned in past discussions: the importance of creating user-friendly, interactive tools that could help clinicians, practitioners, and new researchers better understand data labeling and collection for use in AI.

In closing, Dewji said that this symposium has not only sparked new ideas but also challenged us to think bigger about what is possible. Going forward, it will be important to keep in mind that the future of AI is not just about incremental progress but also about pushing boundaries, reimagining what is possible, and shaping a future where AI works for everyone.

Appendix A
Symposium Agenda

PROGRAM

The symposium will include a community discussion on algorithm development and pathways to success, a focus on future directions and opportunities in AI/ML methods and technology to advance the fields of the radiation health sciences, and discussions on the intentionality of data collection for algorithm development and training, as well as focused breakout sessions on current and emerging applications of AI and ML in the radiation health science fields. Sessions will consider such topics as Broader AI Community Discussions, Future Directions and Opportunities for AI/ML Applications in the Radiation Health Sciences, Data for AI Readiness, AI in the Clinic—Applications in Radiation Oncology and Medical Diagnostics, AI Applications in Occupational and Public Health, and AI Regulations and Ethics.

DAY 1 | THURSDAY, MARCH 13, 2025 (All times are U.S. Eastern)

8:00 AM Call to Order and Welcome
Charles D. Ferguson, National Academies of Sciences, Engineering, and Medicine
Session One | Broader AI Community Discussions

This session aims to engage thought leaders in the broader AI community to share insights from AI developers, users, and government regulators on balancing the benefits of rapid AI innovation and the risks. Talks will address key responsible AI principles in AI model development, human decision making in AI, ethical considerations, and acceptable uncertainty levels for model outputs.

Session Introduction and Overview
Co-moderated by Leo Chiang, Co-Chair, The Dow Chemical Company
Co-moderated by Shaheen Dewji, Co-Chair, Georgia Institute of Technology

8:05 AM Transformational AI Opportunities in Healthcare
David C. Rhew, Microsoft

8:35 AM	The Journey to Safe and Effective AI Adoption Mike Tilkin, American College of Radiology
9:05 AM	Session One | Panel Discussion
9:45 AM	BREAK (10 minutes)

Session Two | Future Directions and Opportunities

This session will explore AI's primary focus areas within each subfield, covering current practices, emerging developments, and challenges to advancing applications. Presenters will discuss both model development and strategic pathways for implementing AI across radiation therapy, diagnostics, occupational health, and environmental safety. The session will emphasize human oversight, ethical considerations, and responsible AI integration to support effective, reliable decision making in these diverse fields.

Session Two A | Future Directions and Opportunities

9:55 AM	Session Introduction and Overview | Radiation Therapy/Oncology Co-moderated by Anyi Li, Planning Committee, Memorial Sloan Kettering Cancer Center Co-moderated by Ceferino Obcemea, Planning Committee, National Cancer Institute
10:00 AM	AI Agents for Adaptive Radiotherapy Steve Jiang, University of Texas Southwestern
10:15 AM	Multi-omics Integration and Pattern Discovery in Patient Data Using Spatially Semantic Topographic Maps Lei Xing, Stanford University
10:30 AM	Session Two A | Panel Discussion Session Two B | Future Directions and Opportunities
11:10 AM	Session Introduction and Overview | Medical Diagnostics Moderated by Caroline Chung, Planning Committee, MD Anderson Cancer Center
11:15 AM	Quantitative MR, Promising Data as a Replacement of CT Cameron Piron, Synaptive Medical
11:30 AM	AI and Quantitative Imaging Jayashree Kalpathy-Cramer, University of Colorado-Anschutz Medical Campus
11:45 AM	Session Two B | Panel Discussion
12:25 PM	LUNCH (1 hour)

Session Two C | Future Directions and Opportunities

1:25 PM	Session Introduction and Overview | AI/ML Innovations in Radiation Occupational Health Moderated by Sylvain Costes, Planning Committee, NASA
1:30 PM	Computational Approaches to Assessing Radiation Exposure Across the Life Course: Risks, Insights, and Innovations Heidi Hanson, Oak Ridge National Laboratory
1:45 PM	Patient-Centric Synthetic Data Generation, No Reason to Risk Re-identification in Biomedical Data Analysis: The Anonymous Synthetic Data Era Pierre-Antoine Gourraud, Nantes Université, University Medical Center (CHU de Nantes), France
2:00 PM	Session Two C | Panel Discussion
2:40 PM	BREAK (10 minutes)

Session Three | Data for AI Readiness

This session will explore the significance of intentional data collection for trustworthy AI model results with a focus on medical imaging as an example. Key topics include data quality and quantity requirements, data collection planning, and data management strategies. Discussion will focus on tackling major gaps, bias, and ethical considerations in radiation health sciences data while suggesting innovative solutions.

2:50 PM	Session Introduction and Overview Co-moderated by Leo Chiang, Co-Chair, The Dow Chemical Company Co-moderated by Anyi Li, Planning Committee, Memorial Sloan Kettering Cancer Center
2:55 PM	Data for AI: The Critical Role of Metadata and Context Caroline Chung, MD Anderson Cancer Center
3:10 PM	Requisites and Challenges in Quantitative Imaging Daniel C. Sullivan, Duke University Medical Center
3:25 PM	Centralized Imaging Collaborations for AI Readiness Paul Kinahan, University of Washington
3:40 PM	Data Management Tools and Strategy for Responsible Imaging AI Daniel Marcus, Washington University School of Medicine in St. Louis
3:55 PM	Session Three | Panel Discussion
4:05 PM	BREAK (10 minutes)

Session Four | Community Discussion and End-of-Day Notes

4:15 PM	Radiation Therapy Wrap-up Report from Anyi Li
4:25 PM	Medical Diagnostics Wrap-up Report from Caroline Chung
4:35 PM	Exposure Assessment Wrap-up Report from Sylvain Costes
4:45 PM	End of Day, Closing Remarks, and Summary on Common Themes Shaheen Dewji
5:00 PM	Adjourn | End of Day 1 of Symposium

Day 2 will provide a platform for invited speakers and participants to present and discuss advancements in AI and ML across diverse areas of radiation science, including health, occupational safety, environmental monitoring, and regulatory frameworks. Moderated panel sessions will build on insights from Day 1's "Future Directions and Opportunities" session, advancing discussions on the application, ethical considerations, and governance of AI across multiple radiation-related fields. This day's agenda will support a comprehensive exploration of AI's role in enhancing radiation safety, data integration, and regulatory processes, fostering collaboration among experts from varied domains within radiation science.

DAY 2 | FRIDAY, MARCH 14, 2025 (All times are U.S. Eastern.)

8:00 AM	Welcome and Overview for Day 2 Leo Chiang, Co-Chair, The Dow Chemical Company Shaheen Dewji, Co-Chair, Georgia Institute of Technology Session Five | Breakout Sessions Five A and Five B

Breakout Session Five A | Location—Fred Kavli Auditorium

8:05 AM	Session Five A | Digital Twins Session Introduction and Overview Co-moderated by Caroline Chung, Planning Committee, MD Anderson Cancer Center Co-moderated by Sylvain Costes, Planning Committee, NASA
8:15 AM	Cardiac Digital Twins: From the Academy to the Clinic Charles A. Taylor, University of Texas at Austin
8:40 AM	Digital Twins for Disease Modeling and Drug Development Jon Walsh, Unlearn

9:05 AM Multiscale Digital Twins for Personalized Radiopharmaceutical Therapy
Greeshma Agasthya, Georgia Institute of Technology

9:30 AM DT and AI for Precision Medicine
Jun Deng, Yale University

9:55 AM Session Five A | Panel Discussion

11:00 AM LUNCH (1 hour)

Breakout Session Five B | Location—NAS 120

8:05 AM Session Five B | AI/ML Applications of Multimodal Modeling
Session Introduction and Overview
Co-moderated by Anyi Li, Planning Committee, Memorial Sloan Kettering Cancer Center
Co-moderated by Ceferino Obcemea, Planning Committee, National Cancer Institute

8:15 AM Integrating Mechanistic Modeling with Machine Learning to Evaluate Radiotherapy and Chemotherapy Outcomes in Head and Neck Cancer
Igor Shuryak, Columbia University Irving Medical Center (CUIMC)

8:40 AM Rapidly Exploring Use Cases for Multimodal AI in Radiology
Nur Yildirim, University of Virginia

9:05 AM Understanding Radiation Risk Through Deep Learning: Promise and Challenges
Zhenqiu Liu, Radiation Effects Research Foundation (RERF), Japan

9:30 AM AI and Multimodal Modeling in Lung Cancer
Jia Wu, MD Anderson Cancer Center

9:55 AM Session Five B | Panel Discussion

11:00 AM LUNCH (1 hour)

Session Six | Breakout Sessions Six A and Six B
Breakout Session Six A | Location—Fred Kavli Auditorium

12:00 PM Session Six A | Ethics and Bias
Session Introduction and Overview
Moderated by Leo Chiang, Co-Chair, The Dow Chemical Company

12:00 PM Artificial Intelligence Preparedness—A Regulatory Perspective
Matt Dennis, U.S. Nuclear Regulatory Commission

12:25 PM Issues in the Use of AI for Breast Cancer Screening
Etta D. Pisano, American College of Radiology

12:50 PM Addressing Bias in AI-Driven Medical Imaging: Pitfalls and Best Practices
Amber Simpson, Queen's University, Canada

1:15 PM Shortcuts Causing Bias in Medical Imaging
Judy Wawira Gichoya, Emory University School of Medicine

1:40 PM Session Six A | Panel Discussion

2:40 PM BREAK (20 minutes)

Breakout Session Six B | Location—NAS 120

12:00 PM Session Six B | Uncertainty Quantification and Trustworthiness
Session Introduction and Overview
Co-moderated by Shaheen Dewji, Co-Chair, Georgia Institute of Technology
Co-moderated by Ceferino Obcemea, Planning Committee, National Cancer Institute

12:00 PM Assessing Uncertainty in Indoor Radon Exposure Estimates: Implications for Radiation Epidemiology
Heidi Hanson, Oak Ridge National Laboratory

12:25 PM Enhancing Trustworthiness: A Case Study on Blood Pressure Modeling with Physics-Informed Neural Networks
Roozbeh Jafari, Massachusetts Institute of Technology Lincoln Laboratory

12:50 PM Jie Yu, Johnson & Johnson

1:15 PM Machine Learning and Low-Field MRI: Unlocking a New Class of Portable Scanners
Matthew Rosen, Harvard Medical School

1:40 PM Session Six B | Panel Discussion

2:40 PM BREAK (20 minutes)

3:00 PM Summary of Symposium and Highlight Discussions
Leo Chiang, Co-Chair
Shaheen Dewji, Co-Chair
Daniel Mulrow, National Academies Symposium Director

3:15 PM Adjourn Symposium | End of Day 2 Symposium

B
Biographies

Greeshma Agasthya (presenter and panelist) is an assistant professor in the Nuclear and Radiological Engineering and Medical Physics Program at the George W. Woodruff School of Mechanical Engineering at Georgia Institute of Technology, where she established the Computational Medical Physics (CoMP) Laboratory in 2024. Dr. Agasthya received her BE in medical electronics from Visvesvaraya Technological University, India (2005), and MS (2011) and PhD (2013) in biomedical engineering at Duke University. She completed her postdoctoral training at the Emory Winship Cancer Institute. The CoMP laboratory, led by Dr. Agasthya, focuses on integrating advanced computational methods, medical physics, and biomedical engineering to personalize medical imaging, radiation therapy, and theranostics. Her research interests are (1) developing multiscale digital twins for personalized radiation dosimetry and outcomes prediction, (2) performing modeling and simulations to assess novel radiation protocols for cancer diagnosis and cancer treatment, and (3) developing artificial intelligence frameworks to model patient trajectories in oncology.

Francis Amankwah (staff member) serves as co-director of the National Cancer Policy Forum and as a senior program officer with the Board on Health Care Services. He has managed consensus study committees and guided those committees in consensus building. He was the responsible staff officer on the National Academies of Sciences, Engineering, and Medicine's consensus study that produced the report *Ending Unequal Treatment: Strategies to Achieve Equitable Health Care and Optimal Health for All*. He served as the responsible staff officer on the National Academies' congressionally mandated consensus study that produced the consensus report *Medications in Single Dose Vials: Implications of Discarded Drugs*. He played an integral role in the development of the National Academies' consensus reports *Guiding Cancer Control: A Path to Transformation* and *Making Medicines Affordable: A National Imperative*. He has also served as the responsible staff officer on numerous workshops and convening activities, and as the rapporteur of several workshop proceedings. He is a recipient of the Health and Medicine Division's Elena Nightingale, Veteran, Mount Everest, and Fineberg staff achievement awards. He earned his MPH and a graduate certificate in global planning and international development from Virginia Tech. He was raised in Ghana, where he earned his BS degree in agricultural science from Kwame Nkrumah University of Science and Technology.

Leo Chiang (planning committee co-chair and session moderator) is a senior research and development (R&D) fellow at Dow Core R&D. He has a broad research interest in emerging artificial intelligence (AI) and data science approaches, and his ambition is to guide the industry to achieve AI at scale. Chiang is a trustee of Computer Aids for Chemical Engineering, the industry co-chair for the 2025 Dynamics and Control of Process Systems conference, and the program chair for the 2026 Foundations of Process/Product Analytics and Machine Learning meeting. He is a fellow of the American Institute of Chemical Engineers and has received much recognition, including the 2016 Herbert Epstein Award, 2016 Computing Practice Award, and American Automatic Control Council 2020 Control Engineering Practice Award. He was elected to the National Academy of Engineering in 2023. Chiang received a BS in chemical engineering from the University of Wisconsin–Madison and an MS and a PhD in chemical engineering from the University of Illinois Urbana–Champaign. He currently serves as a member of the National Academies of Sciences, Engineering, and Medicine's Board on Chemical Sciences and Technology.

Caroline Chung (planning committee member, session moderator, presenter, and panelist) is vice president and chief data and analytics officer, co-director of the Institute for Data Science in Oncology, and a tenured professor in radiation oncology and diagnostic imaging at the University of Texas MD Anderson Cancer Center. Her clinical practice is focused on central nervous system malignancies, and her computational imaging laboratory has a research focus on quantitative imaging and computational modeling to detect and characterize tumors and toxicities of treatment to enable personalized cancer treatment. She is actively involved in multidisciplinary efforts to improve the generation and utilization of quantitative imaging for clinical impact, including as co-chair of the Quantitative Medical Imaging Coalition and co-chair of the Quantitative Imaging for Assessment of Response in Oncology Committee of the International Commission on Radiation Units and Measurements. She is also actively involved in efforts to ensure responsible implementation of technology, including artificial intelligence (AI), in healthcare with roles including as co-chair of the American Society of Clinical Oncology AI Community of Practice as well as member of the new National Institutes of Health Advisory Committee to the Director Working Group on Artificial Intelligence and the National Academies of Sciences, Engineering, and Medicine–appointed Committee on Foundational Research Gaps and Future Directions for Digital Twins. Beyond her clinical, research, and administrative roles, Dr. Chung enjoys serving as an active educator and mentor with a passion to support the growth of diversity, equity, and inclusion in science, technology, engineering, and mathematics, including in her role as chair of Women in Cancer. Chung received an MSc in medical science from the University of Toronto and an MD from the University of British Columbia. She is a fellow of the Royal College of Physicians and Surgeons of Canada.

Sylvain V. Costes (planning committee member and session moderator) was the data officer for the Biological and Physical Sciences Division at National Aeronautics and Space Administration (NASA) Headquarters, under the Science Mission Directorate. He previously served for nearly 8 years as the project manager for NASA's Open Science Data Repository, overseeing the development and management of genetic, epigenetic, proteomic, and physiological data integration. Costes is an expert in radiation biology, co-leading the Radiation Biophysics Laboratory at NASA. He also co-leads the Artificial Intelligence (AI) for Life in Space group, leveraging AI and machine learning methodologies to interpret complex space biology datasets. He has received numerous honors, including the NASA Exceptional Scientific Achievement Medal and the NASA Human Research Program Significant Contributor Award. Costes received a PhD in nuclear engineering, specializing in radiation biology and computational modeling, from the University of California, Berkeley.

Jun Deng (presenter and panelist) is a professor and director of physics research in the Department of Therapeutic Radiology and a professor in the Department of Biomedical Informatics and Data Science at Yale School of Medicine; the principal investigator of Yale Smart Medicine Lab; and the leading member of the Digital Twins for Health Consortium. Dr. Deng received his PhD from University of Virginia and finished his postdoctoral fellowship at Stanford University. With funding from the National Institute of Biomedical Imaging and

Bioengineering, National Science Foundation, National Cancer Institute (NCI), Department of Energy, and Yale College Council, Dr. Deng's research has been focused on artificial intelligence (AI), machine learning, and medical imaging for real-time clinical decision support; digital twins of cancer patients; early cancer detection; as well as AI-empowered mobile health. Dr. Deng is an elected fellow of the Institute of Physics, American Association of Physicists in Medicine, and American Society for Radiation Oncology, and was recently selected as one of the key thought leaders of the NCI Cancer AI Accelerator Program, one of the experts for the National Institutes of Health (NIH) AIM-AHEAD PAIR Program, and one of the mentors for the NIH AIM-AHEAD Research Fellows Program.

Matt Dennis (presenter and panelist) is a data scientist at the U.S. Nuclear Regulatory Commission (NRC) in the Office of Nuclear Regulatory Research, Division of Systems Analysis, and leads the agency's efforts in developing and implementing the NRC Artificial Intelligence Strategic Plan. Additionally, Dennis supports the development and maintenance of the MACCS consequence analysis suite of codes and conducts severe accident consequence analyses. Prior to joining the NRC, Dennis held positions at Northrop Grumman and Sandia National Laboratories. As a senior reliability engineer with the Reliability Analysis Laboratory at Northrop Grumman's Mission Systems Baltimore, he supported sustainment efforts for Global Hawk, Triton, and Phoenix unmanned aircraft systems. As a senior member of the technical staff in the Risk and Reliability Analysis Department at Sandia National Laboratories, Dennis led research and development projects supporting risk assessment and consequence analysis for new and operating nuclear reactors as well as nuclear waste transportation. He has a BS and an MS in nuclear engineering from the Missouri University of Science and Technology.

Shaheen A. Dewji (planning committee co-chair and session co-moderator) is an assistant professor in the Nuclear and Radiological Engineering and Medical Physics Program in the George W. Woodruff School of Mechanical Engineering at the Georgia Institute of Technology. Prior to her current position, she was a faculty member in the Department of Nuclear Engineering at Texas A&M University and a faculty fellow of the Center for Nuclear Security Science and Policy Initiatives. In her preceding role at Oak Ridge National Laboratory, Dewji was a radiological scientist in the Center for Radiation Protection Knowledge. Her recent research has included assessment of patient release criteria for nuclear medicine patients as well as development of dose coefficients associated with the external exposure and internal uptake of radionuclides due to environmental or nuclear security exposures. She was recently appointed to serve on the National Council on Radiation Protection and Measurements PAC-6 as well as the International Commission on Radiological Protection Task Group 127 and Working Party on AI and Radiation Protection, both under Committee 4. Dewji received a BS in physics from the University of British Columbia and an MS and a PhD in nuclear and radiological engineering from the Georgia Institute of Technology. She is an alumna of the Sam Nunn Security Program. She currently serves as a member of the National Academies of Sciences, Engineering, and Medicine's Nuclear and Radiation Studies Board.

Charles D. Ferguson (staff member) is the senior board director of the Nuclear and Radiation Studies Board and the Board on Chemical Sciences and Technology in the Division on Earth and Life Studies at the National Academies of Sciences, Engineering, and Medicine. Previously, he was the president of the Federation of American Scientists (FAS). Prior to FAS, he worked as the Philip D. Reed Senior Fellow for Science and Technology at the Council on Foreign Relations (CFR), where he specialized in nuclear issues, and served as project director for the Independent Task Force on U.S. Nuclear Weapons Policy, chaired by William J. Perry and Brent Scowcroft. Before CFR, he was the scientist-in-residence at the Monterey Institute's Center for Nonproliferation Studies, where he co-authored the book The Four Faces of Nuclear Terrorism (Routledge, 2005) and was lead author of the January 2003 report "*Commercial Radioactive Sources: Surveying the Security Risks*." For his work on security of radioactive sources, he was awarded the Robert S. Landauer Memorial Lecture Award from the Health Physics Society in 2003. He is also the author of "*Nuclear Energy: What Everyone Needs to Know*" (Oxford University Press, 2011). In addition, he has worked as a physical scientist in the Office of Nuclear Safety at the U.S. Department of State, and he has served as a nuclear engineering officer and submarine officer in the U.S. Navy. He is an elected fellow of the American Physical Society in recognition of his service to public policy and public education on nuclear issues. Dr. Ferguson earned a BS in physics with distinction from the U.S. Naval Academy and MA and PhD degrees, also in physics, from Boston University.

Judy Wawira Gichoya (presenter and panelist) is an associate professor at Emory University in interventional radiology and informatics and leads the HITI (Healthcare Artificial Intelligence [AI] Innovation and Translational Informatics) laboratory. Her work is centered on using data science to study health equity. Her group works in four areas—building diverse datasets for machine learning (e.g., the Emory Breast dataset), evaluating AI for bias and fairness, validating AI in the real-world setting, and training the next generation of data scientists (both clinical and technical students) through hive learning and village mentoring. She serves as the program director for radiology, the AI trainee editorial board, and the medical students' machine learning elective. She has mentored more than 60 students (now successful faculty, postdocs, PhDs, and industry employees) from several institutions around the world. She has received several awards including Most Influential Radiology Researcher in 2022 and is a 2023 Emerging Scholar in the National Academy of Medicine.

Pierre-Antoine Gourraud (presenter and panelist) is a university professor, hospital practitioner at the Faculty of Medicine of Nantes University, France. He is an Ecole Normale Supérieure de Lyon's (France) alumni in the Biology Department. He arrived as a post-doctoral researcher from the Department of Neurology at the University of California, San Francisco, and left as an associate professor in 2018. Author of more than 200 publications cited more than 13,000 times (h-index 58), his research activities are at the crossroads of immunology, genetics, and health data processing. Close to the entrepreneurial world, he has been working with several health and biotechnology companies, providing them with the benefit of his expertise.

Heidi Hanson (presenter and panelist) is a senior scientist and group lead of biostatistics and biomedical informatics at Oak Ridge National Laboratory. She is a demographer and life course epidemiologist, with expertise in analysis of population health data. She leads the joint National Cancer Institute (NCI)–Department of Energy Modeling Outcomes Using Surveillance Data and Scalable Artificial Intelligence for Cancer project and the Electronic Health Records–Informed Lagrangian Method for Precisions Public Health: Data-Driven Population Health Surveillance at Scale for Pandemic Readiness project. Her previous projects have taken advantage of large health databases such as NCI's Surveillance, Epidemiology, and End Results, Utah Population Database, Demographic Health Survey, Centers for Medicare & Medicaid Services, and the National Health and Nutrition Examination Survey.

Roozbeh Jafari (presenter and panelist) is a principal staff member in the Biotechnology and Human Systems Division at the Massachusetts Institute of Technology (MIT) Lincoln Laboratory with a joint research appointment on the MIT campus. He is also an adjunct professor in the Department of Electrical and Computer Engineering and in the School of Engineering Medicine at Texas A&M University. Jafari's goal is to establish impactful and highly collaborative programs to promote the health and wellness of interest to our national security and our communities. His aspiration is to serve as a catalyst between Lincoln Laboratory, the MIT campus, and other academic entities across the nation for such programs. He joined MIT from Texas A&M where he was the Tim and Amy Leach Professor in the Department of Electrical and Computer Engineering and in the School of Engineering Medicine. Jafari received his PhD in computer science from the University of California,

Los Angeles, and completed a postdoctoral fellowship at the University of California, Berkeley. His research interests lie in the areas of wearable computer design, sensors, systems, AI for digital health paradigms, and, most recently, digital twin for precision health.

Steve Jiang (presenter and panelist) received his PhD in medical physics from Medical College of Ohio in 1998. After completing his postdoctoral training at Stanford University, he joined Massachusetts General Hospital and Harvard Medical School in 2000 as an assistant professor of radiation oncology. In 2007, Dr. Jiang was recruited to University of California, San Diego (UCSD), as a tenured associate professor to build the Center for Advanced Radiotherapy Technologies, for which he was the founding and executive director. He was then promoted to full professor with tenure in 2011. At UCSD, Dr. Jiang pioneered the use of graphics processing units for healthcare supercomputing, with his team developing more than 40 tool kits to speed up medical imaging and cancer radiotherapy tasks. In October 2013, he joined University of Texas (UT) Southwestern Medical Center as a tenured full professor, Barbara Crittenden Professor in Cancer Research, and vice chair for digital health and artificial intelligence (AI) in the Radiation Oncology Department, as well as director of the Medical Physics and Engineering Division. Dr. Jiang is a fellow of the Institute of Physics, American Association of Physicists in Medicine, and American Institute for Medical and Biological Engineering. His research in various areas of cancer radiotherapy has been funded by federal, state, charitable, and industrial grants for more than $20 million, resulting in more than 200 peer-reviewed journal papers with an H-index of 92. His current research interest is the development and deployment of AI technologies to solve medical problems. He is the founding director of the Medical Artificial Intelligence and Automation Laboratory at UT Southwestern. He has supervised more than 30 postdoctoral fellows and 15 PhD students.

Jayashree Kalpathy-Cramer (presenter and panelist) is the endowed chair in ophthalmic data sciences and the founding chief of the Division of Artificial Medical Intelligence in the Department of Ophthalmology at the University of Colorado School of Medicine. She is also the director for health informatics at the Colorado Clinical and Translational Sciences Institute. She leads the development and translation of novel artificial intelligence (AI) methods into effective patient care practices at the Sue Anschutz-Rodgers Eye Center. Previously, she was an associate professor of radiology at Harvard Medical School and led imaging AI activities as the scientific director at the Massachusetts General Hospital/Brigham and Women's Hospital Center for Clinical Data Science. Her research interests span the spectrum from novel algorithm development to clinical translation. She is actively involved in AI efforts locally and nationally as a senior scientist at the American College of Radiology's Data Science Institute, is on the Artificial Intelligence Committee at the American Academy of Ophthalmology, is a member of the Council of Distinguished Investigators at the Academy for Radiology and Biomedical Imaging Research, and is a deputy editor for the journal *Radiology: Artificial Intelligence*. Dr. Kalpathy-Cramer spent almost a decade in the semiconductor industry before a pivot to academia and healthcare. She has been funded by the National Institutes of Health, National Science Foundation, and the European Union; has co-authored more than 250 peer-reviewed publications; has written more than a dozen book chapters; and is a co-inventor on 15 patents.

Paul E. Kinahan (presenter and panelist) is a professor of radiology and bioengineering and the vice chair of radiology research at the University of Washington in Seattle. He is the head of the Imaging Research Laboratory and clinical director of positron emission tomography (PET)/computed tomography (CT) imaging physics. His research includes optimizing the physics of PET and CT imaging, the use of image reconstruction methods, objective assessment of image quality, and the use of quantitative analysis in imaging-based clinical trials. He was a member of the team that developed the first PET/CT scanner and was a founding member and chair of the

National Cancer Institute's Quantitative Imaging Network and the Quantitative Imaging Biomarkers Alliance. He is a co-principal investigator of the Medical Imaging and Data Resource Center, a multi-society initiative for the collection and dissemination of medical imaging and associated data. He is the co-chair of the Radiological Society of North America's Quantitative Imaging Committee, which has the goal of increasing the use of quantitative imaging biomarkers in clinical practice.

Anyi Li (planning committee member and session co-moderator) is the associate attending physicist and chief of computer service in the Department of Medical Physics at Memorial Sloan Kettering Cancer Center where he leads a team comprising mathematicians, physicists, engineers, and data scientists. Together, they collaborate with the Division of Clinical Physics and the Department of Radiation Oncology to harness artificial intelligence (AI), operational research algorithms, and big data. Their objective is to optimize radiation therapy plans, enhance the efficiency of the radiation treatment process from start to finish, develop a data platform for clinical decision support, and improve patient safety by managing accumulated radiation doses. They utilize the latest language models to analyze clinical event timelines and construct workflow knowledge graphs, which improve the radiation therapy workflow and provide valuable insights to the clinical team. With a background as a theoretical nuclear physicist and research scientist tackling NP-hard (nondeterministic polynomial time) problems, Li transitioned into big data engineering and AI, bringing experience from positions at Yahoo and IBM Watson Health. He received a PhD in theoretical nuclear physics from the University of Kentucky.

Zhenqiu Liu (presenter and panelist) is a senior scientist at the Radiation Effects Research Foundation, with extensive expertise in bioinformatics, computational medicine, and data science. A prolific researcher with more than 150 publications, his current work focuses on advancing machine learning and artificial intelligence methods for low-dose radiation risk assessment. By integrating epidemiological, genomic, and clinical data, his research addresses critical challenges in understanding radiation effects.

Daniel Marcus (presenter and panelist) is a professor of radiology at Washington University School of Medicine and director of the Computational Imaging Research Center, an interdisciplinary team of engineers, scientists, software developers, and informaticists all contributing toward the common goal of enabling imaging in biomedical research. The center develops XNAT, the world's most widely used imaging informatics platform, and contributes to the international biomedical informatics infrastructure through a portfolio of National Institutes of Health–funded projects. Dr. Marcus directs imaging informatics operations for several large-scale research programs, including the Human Connectome Project, the Connectome Coordination Facility, the Dominantly Inherited Alzheimer Network, and the Neuroimaging Informatics and Analysis Center.

Daniel J. Mulrow (staff director) is a program officer of the Nuclear and Radiation Studies Board (NRSB) at the National Academies of Sciences, Engineering, and Medicine. He is the primary staff officer for NRSB's portfolio on radiation health effects and has supported two consensus studies. He serves as the National Academies' program manager for the Radiation Effects Research Foundation Program, a United States–Japan cooperative research institute that investigates the health effects of atomic bomb radiation for peaceful purposes. Additionally, he is staff director of the Gilbert W. Beebe Symposium on Artificial Intelligence/Machine Learning Applications in Radiation Therapy, Diagnostics, and Radiation Occupational Health and Safety. Before the National Academies, Dr. Mulrow worked at the National Nuclear Security Administration for multiple years supporting efforts in stockpile stewardship and strategic partnerships and engagements. He received his PhD in chemistry from Washington University in St. Louis. His research interests included initial studies in ultra-high dose rate (or FLASH) radiation therapy, and the development and characterization of dosimeters and radiation detectors.

Ceferino Obcemea (planning committee member and session co-moderator) is the program director in medical physics at the National Cancer Institute (NCI). He oversees a portfolio of grants that includes all aspects of clinical physics in radiation oncology, novel medical devices, new treatment modalities such as ion beam therapy, online imaging techniques, artificial intelligence (AI) applications in radiotherapy, big data analytics, and machine learning. He also serves as the NCI medical physics liaison to various clinical trial groups comprising the National Clinical Trials Network and to the trans-NCI AI/Machine Learning Working Group, as well as serves as a member of the National Institutes of Health Quantum Information Science Working Group. Prior to NCI, he had many years of experience as chief physicist at Memorial Sloan Kettering Cancer Center, Beth Israel Medical Center, and Georgetown University. He received various research fellowships from the Swedish Institute (Stockholm), Niels Bohr Institute (Copenhagen), International Center for Theoretical Physics (Trieste), and the Quantum Theory Project at the University of Florida, Gainesville, among others. Dr. Obcemea received a PhD in physics from Uppsala University, Sweden, and completed his clinical training at Harvard Medical School. He is board-certified by the American Board of Radiology.

Cameron Piron (presenter and panelist) currently serves as president and co-founder of Synaptive Medical and sits on the board of directors as a chair. He is an industry-recognized leader and innovator in image-guided surgery. Prior to co-founding Synaptive Medical, Piron was president and co-founder of Sentinelle Medical, a medical device company that developed and manufactured advanced magnetic resonance imaging–based breast imaging technologies.

Etta Pisano (presenter and panelist) joined the Advanced Research Projects Agency for Health as portfolio lead overseeing the Advancing Clinical Trials Readiness initiative in March 2024. She also currently serves as the chief research officer at the American College of Radiology and as the principal investigator for the National Cancer Institute–funded, ECOG-ACRIN–sponsored Tomosynthesis Mammographic Imaging Screening Trial, which is comparing digital mammography to tomosynthesis for breast cancer screening and has recruited 108,600 women at 133 centers in the United States, Canada, Argentina, Peru, Italy, Spain, Thailand, Taiwan, and South Korea since it opened in July 2017. She has adjunct faculty appointments in radiology at the University of Pennsylvania and the University of North Carolina (UNC) at Chapel Hill. After completing her undergraduate degree in philosophy at Dartmouth College, Dr. Pisano received her MD from Duke University School of Medicine. She did her radiology residency at Beth Israel Hospital at Harvard Medical School. She next served on the faculty at UNC Medical School where she was founding chief of breast imaging for 16 years before becoming vice dean for academic affairs, overseeing the research and education missions of the medical school. While at UNC, she also served as the first principal investigator for the Clinical and Translational Science Awards grant from the National Center for Advancing Translational Sciences and the founding director of the Biomedical Research Imaging Center. After serving as dean of the College of Medicine and vice president for medical affairs at the Medical University of South Carolina, she joined the faculty of Harvard Medical School, serving as professor in residence at Beth Israel Deaconess Health System from 2015 to 2021. Her career has focused on breast imaging with a special focus on the development and testing of new technologies, most recently studying the application of artificial intelligence and machine learning to breast cancer screening. Dr. Pisano is a member of the National Academy of Medicine and has received gold medals from the Radiological Society of North America, the American Roentgen Ray Society, and the Association of University Radiologists. She is a fellow of the American College of Radiology, the Society of Breast Imaging, and the American Association of Women Radiologists, and she is a member of the International Society for Strategic Studies in Radiology. She also has been recognized by the National Women's History Museum for her accomplishments and has received the Marie Curie Award from the American Association of Women Radiologists.

David C. Rhew (presenter and panelist) is Microsoft's global chief medical officer and vice president of healthcare. He served as Microsoft's international coordinator for the pandemic response, working with the World Health Organization to develop its World Health Data Hub, the Centers for Disease Control and Prevention to stand up their vaccine data lake, and U.S. states to roll-out COVID-19 vaccines. He is an adjunct professor at Stanford University; holds six U.S. technology patents that enable authoring, mapping, and integration of clinical decision support into electronic health records; and has been recognized as one of the 50 most influential clinician executives by Modern Healthcare. Dr. Rhew received his Bachelor of Science degrees in computer science and cellular molecular biology from University of Michigan. He received his MD degree from Northwestern University and completed internal medicine residency at Cedars-Sinai Medical Center. He completed fellowships in health services research at Cedars-Sinai and in infectious diseases at the University of California, Los Angeles. He served as chief marketing officer for Samsung and Zynx Health and sat on the board of the National Quality Forum's Executive Consensus Standards Approval Committee. He is chair emeritus for Consumer Technology Association's Health Technology Board and currently serves on AdvaMed's Digital Health Board; the governing committee for NESTcc, the medical device advisory group for the Food and Drug Administration, the Centers for Medicare & Medicaid Service, and the National Institutes of Health; and the board of directors for Cedars-Sinai Medical Center.

Matthew Rosen (presenter and panelist) is a physicist, tool-builder, and inventor whose research bridges the spectrum from fundamental physics to applied bioimaging work in the field of magnetic resonance imaging (MRI). The Rosen Lab focuses on new methods and tools to enable unconventional approaches to MRI scanner construction. In addition, Dr. Rosen co-directs the Center for Machine Learning at the Martinos Center. He is a fellow of the American Physical Society and the International Society for Magnetic Resonance in Medicine, and was named Distinguished Investigator by the Academy for Radiology and Biomedical Imaging Research in 2023. He is the Kiyomi and Ed Baird MGH Research Scholar, and an associate professor of radiology at Harvard Medical School. He is the founder of five companies including Hyperfine, which has developed the world's first portable MRI scanner that can be used at the patient bedside by virtue of its operation at low magnetic field. He has served on the scientific advisory boards of nine companies since 2014. He is the startup innovation expert for MGB Enterprise Radiology (ERIE).

Igor Shuryak (presenter and panelist) is an associate professor of radiation oncology at the Center for Radiological Research, Columbia University Irving Medical Center. He holds a BA in biology and environmental sciences from Columbia College, an MD from SUNY Downstate Medical Center, and a PhD in environmental health sciences from Columbia University. Dr. Shuryak's research focuses on quantitatively modeling radiation effects, including radiation carcinogenesis, cancer treatment, space radiation effects, and radioresistance. His interdisciplinary background combines proficiency in computational research using mechanistic modeling and machine learning with expertise in biology, medicine, and cancer epidemiology. Dr. Shuryak has received several awards, including the Radiation Research Editor's Award and the Jack Fowler Award from the Radiation Research Society. His current area of interest involves integrating causal machine learning with mechanistic modeling techniques to better understand radiation effects and improve radiotherapy outcomes.

Amber Simpson (presenter and panelist), Canada Research Chair in Biomedical Computing and Informatics at Queen's University, seeks to transform how clinicians treat patients with cancer using a data-driven approach. By defining relevant biomarkers to guide targeted treatments, and ultimately improve human health, she will move the field from the "treat everyone to help a few" paradigm toward precision medicine. Simpson leverages state-of-the-art machine learning technologies for biomedical data integration and exploration—specifically, to develop, validate, and translate to clinical practice two important field innovations. The first will develop benchmarking and novel machine learning–based predictive and prognostic imaging biomarkers to better select patients for optimal treatment. The second innovation will be to integrate computation modeling of multiscale, multi-resolution biomedical data to elucidate new phenotypes, such as appearance, development, and behavior, of cancer tumors.

Daniel Sullivan (presenter and panelist) is professor emeritus, Department of Radiology, at Duke University Medical Center. He completed radiology residency and a nuclear medicine fellowship in 1977 at Yale-New Haven. Dr. Sullivan held faculty appointments at Yale University Medical Center, Duke University Medical Center, and University of Pennsylvania Medical Center, before joining the National Cancer Institute (NCI) at the National Institutes of Health in 1997. From 1997 to 2007, he was associate director in the Division of Cancer Treatment and Diagnosis of NCI and head of the Cancer Imaging Program at NCI. Sullivan is founder and chair emeritus of the Quantitative Imaging Biomarkers Alliance and one of the founders of the Quantitative Medical Imaging Coalition (QMIC). QMIC coordinates a wide range of national and international activities related to the evaluation and validation of quantitative imaging biomarkers for clinical research and practice. His areas of clinical and research expertise focus on improving the use of imaging as a biomarker in clinical trials and clinical practice.

Charles A. Taylor (presenter and panelist) is the W.A. "Tex" Moncrief, Jr., Chair in Computational Medicine in the Oden Institute for Computational Engineering and Sciences, professor in the Department of Internal Medicine, and director of the Center for Computational Medicine at the University of Texas at Austin. Dr. Taylor is also a founder and member of the board of directors of HeartFlow, Inc., a company that provides patient-specific computer models of the coronary arteries for diagnosing and treating heart disease. He was chief technology officer at HeartFlow from 2010 to 2021 and then chief scientific officer from 2021 to 2023. Dr. Taylor is also the chairman of Ebenbuild, GmbH, a company building patient-specific lung digital twins for diagnosing and treating respiratory diseases. Prior to HeartFlow, he was an associate professor in the Departments of Bioengineering and Surgery at Stanford University. He is internationally recognized for his pioneering work over the past 30 years in combining computer simulation methods with medical imaging data for patient-specific modeling of blood flow to aid in the diagnosis and treatment of cardiovascular disease. Dr. Taylor has published more than 450 peer-reviewed journal and conference papers and has more than 300 issued patents worldwide. He received his BS degree in mechanical engineering, MS degree in mechanical engineering, and MS degree in mathematics from Rensselaer Polytechnic Institute; and a PhD in mechanical engineering from Stanford University. Dr. Taylor became a fellow of the American Institute of Medical and Biological Engineering in 2007 and was elected into the U.S. National Academy of Engineering in 2024.

Mike Tilkin (presenter and panelist) is the chief information officer and the executive vice president for technology at the American College of Radiology (ACR). In that capacity, he leads information technology and informatics initiatives that support the broad ACR portfolio, including accreditation, national data registries, education, and clinical research. Mr. Tilkin is engaged in standards and informatics efforts nationally and is responsible for the ACR Data Science Institute, a division of the ACR dedicated to promoting the research, development, and adoption of artificial intelligence in imaging.

Jon Walsh (presenter and panelist) is the co-founder of Unlearn and a scientist passionate about bringing ideas to life and helping teams succeed. He began his career in high-energy physics with a PhD from the University of Washington and a postdoc at University of California, Berkeley, where he worked on modeling and simulating experiments at the Large Hadron Collider. Walsh met his Unlearn co-founders while working as a data scientist at Leap Motion. At Unlearn, Walsh has built technology across data science, machine learning, and statistics, leading and growing several teams across disciplines. He enjoys working with teams to solve challenging problems for customers.

Jia Wu (presenter and panelist) is a tenured associate professor at the MD Anderson Cancer Center, leading a multimodal machine learning laboratory at the intersection of imaging physics, oncology, and computational sciences. His research specializes in machine learning, medical image analysis, and radio-immunogenomics, with a strong focus on developing innovative computational tools to improve cancer prevention, diagnosis, treatment selection, and monitoring. As a principal investigator or co-investigator on multiple National Institutes of Health– and Cancer Prevention and Research Institute of Texas–funded projects, Dr. Wu has made significant contributions to radiomics, pathomics, and radiogenomics, publishing more than 80 peer-reviewed journal articles—more than 40 as a first or senior author. His work has been featured in top-tier journals, including *Lancet Digital Health*, *Nature Machine Intelligence*, *Radiology*, *Cell Reports Medicine*, *The Journal of Pathology*, and *Modern Pathology*. Dr. Wu's research continues to push the boundaries of artificial intelligence–driven oncology, shaping the future of precision medicine.

Lei Xing (presenter and panelist) is the Jacob Haimson and Sarah S. Donaldson Professor and director of the Medical Physics Division of the Radiation Oncology Department at Stanford University School of Medicine. His research has been focused on artificial intelligence in medicine, data science, medical imaging, treatment planning and clinical decision making. Dr. Xing is an author on more than 450 publications in high-impact journals, an inventor/co-inventor on many issued and pending patents, and a co-investigator or principal investigator on numerous grants. He is a fellow of the American Association of Physicists in Medicine (AAPM), the American Society for Radiation Oncology, and the American Institute for Medical and Biological Engineering. He is the recipient of the 2023 Edith Quimby Lifetime Achievement Award of AAPM.

Nur Yildirim (presenter and panelist) is a human–computer interaction (HCI) designer and an assistant professor at the University of Virginia's School of Data Science. Her research focuses on bringing design thinking and participatory approaches to artificial intelligence (AI) innovation to make AI technologies useful in real-world contexts. Yildirim received her PhD from Carnegie Mellon's HCI Institute and spent time at Google Research and Microsoft Research working on human-centered AI innovation. She was named a Rising Star by the Michigan AI Laboratory and the Massachusetts Institute of Technology's Electrical Engineering and Computer Science Department. The National Institutes of Health, the National Science Foundation, and Accenture have supported her work. Before academia, Yildirim worked as a design practitioner in the industry, shipping award-winning products ranging from medical and consumer electronics to assistive robots and toys.

Jie Yu (presenter and panelist) is the head of digital and data science product management at Johnson & Johnson (J&J). He is leading the digital product management team for enterprise functions and driving the digital transformation journey in the supply chain across sectors in J&J, including strategy, portfolio roadmap, and lifecycle management of digital products and solutions. In the meantime, Yu leads the Impact Pillar of J&J's Artificial Intelligence (AI) Council as well as co-chairs the J&J Data Science Community of Practice. Yu has more than 15 years of experience in digital transformation, AI, machine learning, data science, and digital product management. Prior to joining J&J, Yu held various technical and leadership roles at Shell and McMaster University. Yu holds a PhD in chemical engineering with a focus on AI and machine learning from the University of Texas at Austin and a BS in bioengineering from Zhejiang University in China.